FAITH & MONEY

$

UNDERSTANDING ANNUAL GIVING IN CHURCH

MICHAEL REEVES AND JENNIFER TYLER

DISCIPLESHIP RESOURCES

PO BOX 340003 • NASHVILLE, TN 37203-0003
www.discipleshipresources.org

Cover and book design by Joey McNair

Edited by Linda R. Whited and Heidi L. Hewitt

ISBN 0-88177-410-3

Library of Congress Control Number 2003106215

DR410

Contents

Acknowledgments

Considering the laws of success, it is implied that every product or service must be different and better in some extraordinary way to gain an edge. Stewardship, both as a product and as a service, provides us with numerous uncommon opportunities to reach new personal and professional heights.

We continue to be inspired and challenged by our colleagues, clients, and contemporaries who, like us, have dedicated most of their adult lives to pursuing advancement in stewardship and in various other areas of ministry. As we collaborate to blaze new trails of thought about stewardship and innovative, yet down-to-earth, ways to teach stewardship, our desire is that the integrity of it all be found in solidly rooted, time-tested, biblical principles.

We particularly wish to thank Sanford Coon for his abiding friendship and remarkable insight into many aspects of stewardship. You will see his influence especially in the portion of the book that deals with ways and means for communicating stewardship to people of all ages—and throughout the book for that matter. His collaborative efforts contributed greatly toward enabling us to reach our content goals. Also, unlimited appreciation goes to the people of each of our respective organizations whose assistance and encouragement along the way enabled us to complete this task.

Finally, we must without fail and with great devotion express appreciation to our families, whose understanding, patience, and long suffering have enabled us to do what we do.

Michael Reeves and Jennifer Tyler

Introduction

O ne of the greatest challenges facing the church in the twenty-first
century is knowing how to understand and effectively address the
connection between faith and money. Unfortunately, this connection
is most often communicated as the church's need for funding (commonly
labeled *stewardship*). A disconnection of heretical proportion exists between
theology and practice in the area of faith and money. Over the last thirty-five
years, North America has experienced the greatest increase of discretionary
income in the history of the world. During this time, churches have looked
for the quickest fix for funding the budget, with little regard to developing an
effective theology of stewardship consistent with heritage, Scripture,
tradition, and practice.

The common response of church members to stewardship efforts reflect
the problem: "I don't like so much talk about money." Some say that they do
not care for "preaching about money." Others say that we ought not teach
about money in small groups that are supposed to be for fellowship. Many
express a lack of regard for receiving mail about church finances: "If they
had their act together, they would mail me stuff only once a month. It is just
a waste of money to mail all that stuff." Others express negative feelings
about phone calls regarding stewardship, since they often already receive too
many telemarketing calls. The most disconcerting remarks concern the

confrontational nature of home visits during stewardship efforts: "Nobody wants to make or receive one of those kinds of visits." So, the rules seem to be that the church should "find a way to raise the budget without talking, teaching, preaching, writing, calling, or visiting about money."

Not long ago a newly appointed senior pastor in a large suburban church stood on a Sunday morning in October and opened his message by saying, "I have been told that this is the Sunday for the annual stewardship sermon. I don't like preaching about this, and I know that you don't like hearing about it. But the leaders felt that it had to be done; so if you will be patient with me, I will finish this as soon as I can." The implication was that the subject was not only distasteful but also adjunctive to important spiritual issues. The pious assertion that "we don't talk about money," as if it were a commendable statement, should be called what it is: heresy. To really understand the problem requires seeing things in a fundamentally different way from what has become commonplace in the church. We have the wrong perspective because we have the wrong leaders, who have the wrong gifts, ask the wrong questions, and make the wrong assumptions. The way we report our finances is wrong, our timing in addressing the subject is wrong, our methods are wrong, and our basic thinking is wrong.

The starting point for developing a clear understanding of the real challenge we face is found in the words of Jesus in Matthew 6:24: "No one can serve two masters; for a slave will either hate the one and love the other, or be devoted to the one and despise the other. You cannot serve God and wealth." The issue is not funding a church budget; the issue is determining who we serve.

A number of excellent books and resources have been developed in recent years that address various considerations of stewardship. Often, the texts include topics such as stewardship of time, spiritual gifts, ecology, prayer, and others under the conceptual umbrella of holistic stewardship. Certainly, a healthy theology of stewardship would consider all of creation. However, such definitions are not the purpose of this book. More research and analysis about money and church are probably available now than ever before, but the church continues to decline in most measurements of financial support. Wonderful exceptions exist; but in an age of affluence in North America, most churches struggle to fund ministries and even meet basic obligations of fixed overhead. When limited resources dictate a limited vision for the church, money becomes a critical issue.

This book will begin to identify the real challenges, a consistent theological foundation, and worthy expectations and attitudes and how to develop them. I will discuss leadership, along with general approaches that are consistent with sound theology. Ideas that really work will be presented in a context of an intentional design beyond the incidental raising of funds for the church budget. Every effort will be made to reframe faith and money as a core spiritual value worthy of consideration, instead of as an adjunctive evil necessary only for paying bills. The purpose of this book is to challenge prevailing attitudes and practices by developing an understanding of faith and money that reflects the gospel of Christ.

Chapter One

Challenges

We face substantial challenges to making the connection between faith and money. The challenges include cultural, historical, traditional, emotional, financial, ecclesiastical, and theological issues. Making the connection requires a fundamental change in the way we think. The momentum of perspective created by these kinds of issues concerning faith and money must be redirected before a healthy connection can be made. It is not a matter of what new idea we employ to address the subject, although new ideas may help. It is first a matter of appreciating the multitude of challenges that we must address.

Cultural Challenges

We first need to appreciate the culture we have developed in North America. Based on free enterprise, capitalism has conditioned the way we value material goods. The distinction can be seen when observing the differences between graduate theological students from North America, Asia, and Africa. These students view money and possessions in radically different ways. For instance, while North American students often express reservations about the value of tithing as a goal, foreign students embrace without reservation the biblical standard as a threshold of giving. While students from North America tend to dress better, drive better cars, and carry more debt, foreign students consistently establish and live with a lower standard of materialism. In North America, we find no irony when political leaders suggest that the way we can improve our economy is to consume more, despite record numbers of personal bankruptcies and escalating personal debt. In North America, we have come to a time in our culture when we cannot answer the question of how much is enough. We have seen this truth recently in shameful and embarrassing examples of corporate greed. Perspective seems to be lost when executives feel entitled to millions of dollars in compensation while their companies lose billions of dollars, go bankrupt, and cannot fund retirement programs. In this culture, making a connection between faith and money is extremely challenging.

Historical Challenges

Historically, we are the beneficiaries of the greatest explosion of discretionary wealth in the history of the world. In the last fifty years, an unusual economic reality has developed. We have come to a time when we define the good life in a context of accumulation. Unfortunately, it seems that many churches and church leaders are more driven by market values in church program and ministry than by a sense of countercultural spiritual purposes. It is in this context that we have made a transition in church life about financial stewardship. The issue of financial stewardship was a matter of common discourse from biblical times until the mid-twentieth century. Steward was a term of respect used to refer to mature leaders. The discussion about money seemed to be easier when people had less discretionary income. We have replaced that sense of openness with a conspiracy of silence, where any discussion about faith in regard to money seems out of place. Money is more often spoken about with regard to need and limitation. The silence about personal stewardship seems to be countered only with appeals for financial support, instead of with open discussion, teaching, preaching, and encouragement about the issues of consumption, saving, management, and generosity.

Traditional Challenges

A tradition of silence and unspoken expectation seems to have developed, which complicates effective communication. For instance, many church leaders believe that money matters should be addressed only when absolutely necessary in times of funding shortfalls. And although the pastor should be equipped to address such personal issues as marital relations, ethical dilemmas, moral failures, and even criminal acts, many believe that pastors cannot be trusted to discuss financial issues with their members. The idea that clergy cannot be trusted with knowledge of how people give suggests that there is no spiritual connection to money. The thought that clergy would treat donors or non-donors differently is a humanistic view that seems to suggest that personal finances and giving are not spiritual issues that ought to be addressed. But that view has complications. If a family is giving a significant amount of money to a church and then stops, that action suggests that something has happened in that family. The family members may have experienced an economic loss or lost their passion about the church. That would suggest that a spiritual need be addressed. Or the inverse could be equally true. If a person who had no record of consistent giving begins to give consistently or at a substantial level, something has apparently happened in that person's spiritual journey. Would it not be of interest to the pastor to know what happened? How does a church determine the appropriate leadership for financially oriented committees, without some knowledge of personal stewardship? Would it not be more effective to have financial leaders who are donors? Unfortunately, our recent tradition often seems to overlook spiritual connections to giving money.

Emotional Challenges

Of course, connecting faith and money has some emotional challenges as well. Many clergy and lay leaders feel inadequate and genuinely fear addressing the subject. This fear is sometimes fueled by a lack of knowledge of a sound theology of stewardship. Not only do they lack training in the area of finances but many also began their ministry in debt with school and seminary loans, and some attempt to live a lifestyle comparable to their church members without the same income level. It is hard to address financial issues when you face personal debt, financial failure, and lack of training. And church leaders and clergy do not want to do something that is often interpreted as unpopular. They have a legitimate fear about offending people and causing them to leave the church. Of course, logic would suggest that those most easily offended would likely be those who give the least.

Financial Challenges

The challenge in connecting faith and money has a great deal to do with financial realities. A mountain of evidence indicates that average Americans carry more debt than ever, save less than ever, and tend to consistently spend more than they earn. One of the reasons for these financial challenges is the marketing strategies used in our consumer culture, which is designed to provide immediate gratification. Marketers know that spiritual values are important, so they have included some of them in how they market products. Advertisements offer us things such as world harmony, something real, something that is true, no sacrifice, peace of mind, love, nurture and protection, sex appeal, success, purity, lifetime memories, and the list goes on and on. Lost in this market message is that God can make a difference in lives—but not through stuff. This financial challenge seems to transcend generational differences, too. Mounting evidence shows that senior adults sixty-five years or older have more reliance on debt than ever before.

Ecclesiastical Challenges

A significant disconnect seems to exist ecclesiastically between faith and money. An example of this is the use of a line-item budget in communicating ministry objectives. This type of budget complicates the task of communicating the mission and vision of the church. Practice does *not* make perfect; it only makes permanent what you practice. A line-item budget has seldom elicited a positive passion. Church members tend to understand the mission of the church from the microcosm of their own involvement. The big picture of all that the church does in a community is often not communicated in a way that allows the members to move out of that microcosm understanding. Also, there is a gross lack of understanding about how the Bible connects faith and money. The Bible has more verses about a person's relationship to possessions and giving than about prayer, believing, and love combined. As a matter of fact, Jesus spent a third of the parables addressing the subject. The relevance of what the Bible suggests to us about money is often not presented as an issue of discipleship at all.

Theological Challenges

The lack of biblical understanding leads to the challenge of the lack of a sound theology of stewardship. Although the Bible addresses the subject of stewardship throughout the Old and New Testament—and despite the rich heritage of sermons and teaching by church leaders such as John Wesley throughout history—we have not begun to address developing a theology of stewardship until recent years. Instead of requesting that seminaries develop a course on theology of stewardship, perhaps a more theologically relevant approach would be to integrate stewardship into biblical, historical, moral, and systematic theology courses. Raising the level of theological discourse could begin to redirect our thoughts and perspectives on issues of faith and money.

The challenges to making the connection between faith and money seem to be almost overwhelming. And unless we begin to make some fundamental changes, we are likely to perpetuate the poor results we have experienced. The reality is that we have more resources than ever before, but we share fewer of them. In an age of increased prosperity, it is easy to express faith in material gain and accumulation, rather than in the pursuit of holiness. That tendency represents an enormous challenge.

For Further Study

Behind the Stained Glass Windows: Money Dynamics in the Church, by John and Sylvia Ronsvalle (Baker Books, 1996).

Creating a Climate for Giving, by Donald W. Joiner (Discipleship Resources, 2001).

The Crisis in the Churches: Spiritual Malaise, Fiscal Woe, by Robert Wuthnow (Oxford University Press, 1997).

How Much Is Enough? Hungering for God in an Affluent Culture, by Arthur Simon (Baker Books, 2003).

"Identifying and Overcoming Obstacles to Stewardship," Chapter 3 in *Creating Congregations of Generous People,* by Michael Durall (Alban Institute, 1999).

The Index of Leading Spiritual Indicators, by George Barna (Word Publishing, 1996).

Plain Talk About Churches and Money, by Dean Hoge, Patrick McNamara, and Charles Zech (Alban Institute, 1998).

Chapter Two

A Theology of Stewardship

S everal excellent books and articles have been written to address subjects such as the biblical foundations of stewardship and tithing and the theological foundations of stewardship. This chapter is not intended to be an exhaustive treatise on *the* theology of stewardship, nor is it intended to be a comprehensive consideration such as you might find in a book on that topic. The intent of this chapter is to establish a starting point for developing a theology of stewardship.

Biblical Foundations

One approach to considering a theology of stewardship is to review the biblical story through creation, captivity, deliverance, covenant, judgment, redemption, incarnation, resurrection, and Pentecost. The subjects could include time, possessions, spiritual gifts, the gospel, ecology—indeed, all of creation. The biblical perspectives could also be narrowed to include creation, exodus, exile, grace, and eschatology. One of the problems in addressing a theology of stewardship is that the Bible offers so much information that there is a tendency to simplify the biblical basis using a few verses out of context to support a point, or at least an inconsistent biblical criticism.

The rich biblical text is reflected in a biblical concordance, including such words as *generosity, generous, gift, gifts, give, giving, greed, money, offering,*

poor, possessions, poverty, rich, riches, sacrifice, stewards, tithe, and *wealth.*
The biblical text can be used to ground a theology of stewardship, or it can
be used to connect faith and money through simple biblical observation.
Various passages of Scripture dealing with topics such as the significance
and place of God (Exodus 20:3 and Deuteronomy 6:5), lifestyle and priorities
(Romans 12:1-2; Philippians 1:27; Colossians 3:1-2), motivations of the
heart (1 Chronicles 29:9; Matthew 6:21; 2 Corinthians 9:7), and
disproportionate giving by the poor (Mark 12:38-44 and 2 Corinthians 8:1-5)
have all served to establish starting points for a theology of stewardship. With
one-third of the parables addressing the subject of possessions, more than
2,000 verses on the subjects mentioned above, and only the kingdom of God
being addressed by Jesus more than the subject of our possessions, it is ironic
that connecting faith and money is often overlooked in theological studies.
(See pages 103–125 for a list of selected passages related to stewardship.)

The Tithe

Tithing is the most prevalent biblical theme used to address stewardship.
It is first mentioned in Genesis 14:20, but it is not unique to the Old
Testament or to Mosaic law. Tithing has been found as a key principle in the
history of the Arabians, Carthaginians, Lydians, Assyrians, Babylonians,
Greeks, Romans, and Mohammedans.

Three kinds of tithes are mentioned in the Old Testament. Leviticus
27:30-32 describes the standards for tithes that are given to support the
priesthood. The second kind of tithe, which supports some Jewish festivals of
thanksgiving, is found in Deuteronomy 12:5-19 and 14:22-27. In
Deuteronomy 14:28-29 and again in 26:12-15, a third tithe was taken every
third year for the needy. This system of tithes represents an annual average of
$23^{1}/_{3}$% of income in a given three-year time period, but the more important
observation is that the tithe was a standard used for commutation.

The challenge with the tithe is whether tithing is a relevant standard for
today. When graduate theological students consider this question, Asian and
African students have little problem with the tithe; but North American
students often struggle to find tithing relevant in their ministries and life.
From a larger observation in North America, research generally indicates that
the larger the adjusted gross income, the smaller the percentage of charitable
contribution. In other words, when we have more, we tend to give less of it.

Several arguments can be made against the tithe as a relevant issue today.
For instance, some suggest that tithing is not mentioned in the New
Testament, although it is passively affirmed in Matthew 23:23; Luke 11:42;

Luke 18:12; and Hebrews 7:4-9. Another defensive attitude is that tithing is legalistic, belongs to one denomination more than another, or remains a virtue held only by more theologically conservative communities of faith. One of the most frequently-asked irrelevant questions is whether the tithe should be determined on the gross or net of income. The real question here seems to be what the bare minimum legal requirement might be. None of these arguments succeeds in proving that the tithe is no longer a relevant standard for giving.

A Theology of Stewardship

The question of establishing a starting point for an adequate theology of stewardship is presented from the perspective of revelatory theology. God continues to make relevant revelation as we grow in our faith and spiritual maturity closer to God. From that perspective consider these theological principles as a starting point to express a meaningful theology of stewardship:

- *God is the source, and giving is rooted in God.* When working out a theology of stewardship, practical thinking might lead us to consider affluent individuals as the real source of funding for ministry. Professional consultants might be considered rainmakers for generating new streams of revenue. The right software or technology to record and analyze funding might be disproportionately valued in daily administration. Even methodology, such as direct mail or fundraising events, might be considered as prime sources for generating money. All of these variant issues can have some relevance in how we consider money, but the recognition that God created and owns everything is the appropriate starting point for understanding a theology of stewardship.
- *The Bible offers one standard of measurement in our response: the tithe.* We live in an age where the phrase *fair share* is valued as politically correct, but the Bible offers the tithe. Some churches have used assessments that are related to a host of variables to establish expectations, but the Bible offers the tithe. With ever-expanding ministries and programs, some churches rely on user fees to pay for some ministries, but the Bible offers the tithe. Throughout the Old Testament, we find the story of God's people establishing their own standards in conflict with God's standards. Our nature has not changed much in this regard.
- *Giving is indispensable to Christian discipleship.* We express our priorities, values, and love by our giving. Giving also connects people with mission. The prevalent belief for many years has been that as church members

mature in their faith, they will somehow begin to understand and value giving as an expression of that faith. However, the evidence does not validate this view. A more accurate view is that giving is a part of the process that helps people mature in their expression of faith.

- *Ministry should be funded, but claiming rights to funding does not mature believers or reflect Christian theology.* The spirit of entitlement is ultimately an expression of self-righteousness. A stronger theological position is to be thankful for funding as God's provision and to thank those who give.
- *A theology of stewardship should include an expectation of necessary funding of needs.* The thought that God will provide for our needs is basic to our belief system. The implication is that we should avoid negative communication, such as "poor" talk, including whining, negative attitudes, and petty jealousy. Celebrate the positive, the encouraging, and the praiseworthy.
- *The focus of our conversations about giving should be on a person's need to give as a part of personal spiritual growth and discipleship,* rather than on the reality of affluence or poverty. Too often we want those church members who have a large measure of financial wealth to be the financial leaders, but the issue ought to focus on their spiritual maturity expressed by their giving. When churches identify those who express the gift of giving in their community of faith, it is common to find people of modest resources included in the top levels of giving.
- *We should embrace and share the greatness of the vision of the church with passion and excitement.* Unfortunately, we have often approached stewardship by discussing issues surrounding financial need.
- *Giving includes more than the product of our labor, for it is not just a pocketbook decision.* Giving is a volitional decision of the heart, an expression of gratitude and love for God.

In addition to these simple starting points of consideration, a theology of stewardship might include a denominational heritage or a church's relationships beyond itself for missions. However, these more general observations about giving will guide the subsequent consideration of faith and money in this book.

For Further Study

Afire With God: Spirit-ed Stewardship for a New Century, by Betsy Schwarzentraub (Discipleship Resources, 2000).

A Christian View of Money: Celebrating God's Generosity, by Mark Vincent (Herald Press, 1997).

"Developing a Theology of Funding Ministry," Chapter 3 in *Creating a Climate for Giving,* by Donald W. Joiner (Discipleship Resources, 2001).

Generous Saints: Congregations Rethinking Ethics and Money, by James Hudnut-Beumler (Alban Institute, 1998).

Giving From a Wesleyan Perspective, by Kenneth L. Carder, in the kit *Wesley and Giving* (United Methodist Communications, 1998). Phone: 888-346-3862 (item #843433).

Growing Givers' Hearts: Treating Fundraising as Ministry, by Thomas H. Jeavons and Rebekah Burch Basinger (Jossey-Bass, 2000).

Holy Smoke! Whatever Happened to Tithing? by J. Clif Christopher and Herb Mather (Discipleship Resources, 1999).

The Passionate Steward: Recovering Christian Stewardship From Secular Fundraising, by Michael O'Hurley-Pitts (St. Brigid Press, 2001).

Stewards in the Kingdom: A Theology of Life in All Its Fullness, by R. Scott Rodin (InterVarsity Press, 2000).

That's What My Mother Taught Me (and Other Ways Generous Givers Develop), by Herb Mather (Discipleship Resources, 2001).

Chapter Three

Worthy Goals and Expectations

The next logical step in the development and expression of a theology of stewardship is the definition of worthy goals and expectations. We have all met people with great resources and little interest in giving, as well as others who have extremely generous spirits but few resources from which to give. Have you ever wondered what motivates people to give? What are the spiritual values that guide issues in faith and money and ultimately lead to setting worthy goals?

The Bible: The Beginning Point

The beginning point for setting worthy goals and expectations can again be found in the Bible. Our foremost mandate as followers of Christ is to build up the body of Christ. While there are many important aspects of this, one irrefutable way to advance the Kingdom is through giving. Giving takes us to new spiritual levels and matures us in our faith. Philippians 1:27 reveals a fundamental guideline:

> Only, live your life in a manner worthy of the gospel of Christ, so that, whether I come and see you or am absent and hear about you, I will know that you are standing firm in one spirit, striving side by side with one mind for the faith of the gospel.

God's Expectations

In order to set worthy goals, we must embrace our personal responsibility to understand the expectations God has of us, whether lay or clergy. Two familiar, frequently-referenced resources for discovering these expectations are 2 Corinthians 8–9 and Philippians 4. In these passages, we learn that our giving sets off a chain reaction of three things.

• *First, when we give, needs are met.* Each year, the church forecasts planned ministries. The church family is asked to prayerfully embrace the church's missional goals and to make a faith commitment to return God's tithes and their offerings to support these ministries. By making such commitments, members help assure that the message of Christ can be told. The invitation to give is a call to action. Contrary to what some think, there is no neutral position. Either we give or we do not. When we fail to respond, we are not simply saying no to the church, we are saying no to God. When church leaders are afraid of teaching the biblical standard of giving as a vital discipleship life emphasis, the people in the pew are robbed of a biblical truth that can engender spiritual growth that deepens with time.

• *Second, when we give, our sacrifice is "pleasing to God" (Philippians 4:18).* Considering that more than one-third of what Jesus said during his brief ministry on earth related to giving and possessions as keys to the Kingdom, it is safe to say that faithful stewardship is important. God's work waits upon the faithfulness of God's people. How long must it wait?

• *Third, when we give, we are blessed: "And my God will fully satisfy every need of yours according to his riches in glory in Christ Jesus" (Philippians 4:19).* Some people shy away from talking about the immeasurable blessings associated with giving. Those seeking to profit with their sow-a-seed-of-faith message and receive unprecedented return have long abused this principle. When the donor does not experience windfall profits, he or she is told that it is a result of weak faith. It is a well-documented biblical truth that when we give liberally to God, we are the recipients of a promise that the Lord will give liberally to us. God provides for those who trust enough to give liberally. Teaching people that they would receive financial rewards for giving has always felt uncomfortable. Teach them instead to give because of their love for the Lord. But, if we teach what the Bible says on the subject, just about every time the Bible commands us to give, it is accompanied by a promise of reward to the giver. It is impossible to teach the whole biblical truth on giving without reference to this fact. A few examples can be found in Proverbs 3:9-10; Proverbs 11:24-25; Malachi 3:10; Luke 6:38; and 2 Corinthians 9:6.

The Importance of Faith and Prayer

Setting worthy goals requires faith. We hear the Bible promises and think, *I believe; but given my situation, these Scriptures on giving probably don't apply to me.* We sometimes feel an uncomfortably wide gap between what the Lord says and what we really feel about giving. We know that everything God says is true and, because of our faith, want to accept it. However, some of the verses on giving clash with our humanness and conflict with our economics, and our faith gets a little shaky on the subject of giving. God respects our desire to believe. One day a man who was struggling with his faith said to Jesus, "I believe; help my unbelief!" (Mark 9:24). Prayer is an essential part of setting worthy goals.

Leaders Lead the Way

Leading God's people to embrace the need to set worthy goals while modeling such goals should be among the top priorities of the church. In order to lead the congregation to set worthy goals, clergy and church leaders must be trained and equipped to know what the Bible says about giving. They must embrace its truths at personal levels. It is unlikely that church leaders can lead and effectively influence others to do what they are unwilling to do themselves, or to value something that they do not value. The cardinal rule of stewardship remains: Leaders give first. King David best modeled this concept in 2 Chronicles 29 by his own generous giving to provide for the building of the Temple.

All too often, the person in the pew becomes turned off and alienated by constant talk of budgets and money. Failure to connect money with missional goals and spiritual precepts perpetuates the cycle of poverty with regard to available funds for ministry. Show me a church that talks about money all the time, and I will see a church that never has enough funding to go around.

A pastor of a sizable urban church told me that he took a different approach in the church's annual fall appeal for stewardship: "I actually preached a series of sermons on stewardship, laying out the challenges and biblical expectations, and the congregation responded by committing more tithes and offerings than ever before in the history of the church." Rarely do we find expectations for a great missional vision communicated as the underpinning for the church's annual budget drive. Instead, the message often is, "The church needs your money." Mission, ministry, and discipleship are often effectively masked in the presentation of dollars and cents. Tell the people what the Scriptures say about giving so that they will recognize the truth when they hear it and will have a chance to grow spiritually as a result.

When Leaders Do Not Lead

Unfortunately, many clergy view financial issues as the most dreaded part of the job. One pastor said with great pleasure that the church board told him when he came to the church that he would never have to talk about money. Months later, when the church's ministry obligations were not being met, the church board suggested that the pastor preach on stewardship. He was highly offended by the thought. The pastor had probably not personally embraced giving; otherwise, talking about the joys of giving would have been second nature. While it is surprising to find clergy who do not give, it is even more surprising to have laypeople tell about it. Though financial records for the most part are confidential, word leaks out. When clergy are not trained or equipped to address the subject of money, it becomes adjunctive to core spiritual values, rather than an integral part of the Christian message.

If stewardship is frightening, the pastor's view becomes, *What is the least I can do for the maximum response from the congregation?* This often leads to a watered-down, cafeteria-style approach to setting and acting on worthy goals. This multiple-choice, cafeteria concept for stewardship seems to indicate that if one cannot give money, then one can give time or something else in lieu of finances. One fundamental truth that is missing from this concept is that God expects us to give the first of our material possessions, not the dregs. The Christian view is that we give to God first, and then we regulate our expenditures according to what is left—not first satisfy our needs and wants and then give if anything is left over (Proverbs 3:9). Presenting giving and financial issues as one of many other aspects of stewardship is fine; but, ultimately, giving money must be brought clearly into focus, and the challenge to give must be made. The challenge becomes an impetus to act on the worthy goals that we have set. Church leaders have a huge responsibility to present the message of stewardship with passion and conviction. The church cannot get beyond where it is today, or even maintain its current position, without it.

Some stewardship resources seem to present a one-size-fits-all view. Giving is relegated to a one-dimensional process, with little emphasis on how the corporate giving of the church enables lives to be changed for Christ. When we fail to embrace giving as a core spiritual value and to equip leaders on the subject, we should not be surprised when funds are not available for ministry.

Some leaders may think that we must exert pressure on the clergy to support stewardship needs, but this is a confrontational attitude. What is missing are clearly defined, worthy expectations that are communicated with passion and compassion, goals that would inspire clergy to rise up in faith and answer the call. Whether an individual, congregation, or denomination, who among us would not like to have more resources available to do the things we want to do? Few churches do not need more funding to accomplish their missional purposes. The message of stewardship and setting worthy goals should come from the top and radiate throughout the congregations.

Recently, a friend shared a letter her pastor had sent out to the entire congregation. The letter told of the church's dire financial straits, which have led to layoffs and cutbacks in ministries and services. The letter used strong language to present the financial shortfall, cast in the economic times in which we live. The letter told about the job cuts, but it was uninspired about action. It lacked substance and inspiration, though the language had spiritual connotations. Such an appeal would hardly rally the troops to hang tough spiritually and remain faithful in giving, trusting God for the future. The closing call to prayer appeared as an afterthought.

The result of these varied views gives way to a recurring cycle of church poverty, acceptable whining about a need, and an acquiescence that the church may survive but will never thrive. The church's need becomes in essence the opposite side of our own personal poverty, a mirror image of the self-imposed limitations we set for ourselves. Worthy goals and personal expectations rooted in spiritual matters are missing.

Inspired to Give

When a church models faithfulness and wise management of entrusted funds, it sends a positive message to congregants to do likewise. When a church turns inward and its goals largely relate to self-serving needs, it encourages congregants to do the same. The next time your congregation is invited to support a worthy ministry goal beyond the local church, think about the value it brings to the overall spiritual health and well-being of the church. God has placed resources within the congregation to get the job done. Church leaders must model and inspire worthy goals. Most congregations are still waiting for the message to come from the pulpit, as it did to the Israelites building the tabernacle: "Stop giving, we have enough!" When this biblical example is mentioned in stewardship meetings, it always brings incredulous laughter from the audience, as there is no way on earth that they can possibly envision this fairy tale happening in their church.

Speaking of worthy goals and expectations, what do you suppose drove those former Israelite slaves to reach this unbelievable level of giving? Obviously, they were inspired by the worthy goal of seeing the tabernacle built by the faithfulness of their hands, coupled with their love of God. When we stop talking about money and talk about how people's lives are being changed forever because of hearing the gospel, hearts will be stirred and giving will be inspired. When God has done so much for us, it is only proper that we should be ill at ease unless we respond. It is healthy when we find it impossible to enjoy our own accommodations while the community cannot be properly served because of lack of facilities or ministries.

Worthy Goals for Giving

In setting worthy goals for giving, two essential ingredients—two expectations—please God.

- *First, in order to be truly worthy, our goals should reflect the best we can offer.* To offer God less than our best is to despise God's name. While that may sound a little strong, listen to Malachi as he spoke to those who were offering God less than their best:

> O Priests, who despise my name. You say, "How have we despised your name?" By offering polluted food on my altar. And you say, "How have we polluted it?" By thinking that the LORD's table may be despised. When you offer blind animals in sacrifice, is that not wrong? And when you offer those that are lame or sick, is that not wrong? Try presenting that to your governor; will he be pleased with you or show you favor?   (Malachi 1:6-8)

- *The second expectation is that acceptable, worthy goals and giving come from the first fruits:* "Honor the LORD with your substance and with the first fruits of all your produce" (Proverbs 3:9). Self-survival is a strong instinct that can be overshadowed only by willful faith. God measures our gifts not in relation to what others give but by what we have left over.

Chapter Four

Leadership

S everal leadership roles impact financial decisions in a church. The pastor, treasurer, finance committee members, financial secretary, and even significant donors all have influence that can affect how the church manages, reports, and views money. Some traditions have created a momentum that has not served the church well. The momentum is to do what has always been done in developing a church budget, reporting church finances, and separating money issues from faith issues. This style is seen in who is enlisted to serve, how they are trained, and the basic understanding of the scope of their responsibilities. Doing what has always been done is a serious systemic problem that must be acknowledged and addressed if we hope to have a different, more positive experience with faith and money.

The biblical story of the twelve spies sent by Moses into the Promised Land in Numbers 13 is a good illustration of the impact of leadership attitudes. Those who brought the negative report saw the obstacles as insurmountable, despite the promises of God. The minority report by Caleb and Joshua was positive, acknowledging the challenges but expressing confidence that the challenges could be overcome. What was the result of the divided report and the negative majority? Some called for new leadership and even a return to slavery. The negative majority did not encourage hope or engage hearts. To achieve better results, we have to think more like those who brought the positive report. We must also enable and encourage the perseverance of the voice of the positive minority report.

Clergy as Leaders

The new thinking must start with the clergy. For too long, pastors have seen faith and money as an adjunctive issue to the core spiritual issues of pastoral leadership. They have this perspective for several reasons. First, they were not trained in theological studies in issues of faith and money. It was not a separate course at seminary and was not integrated into their systematic theology course. They did not have any resources or encouragement in this area in their ordination or in any facet of their training and preparation for ministry. Second, they are the beneficiaries of an oral tradition in the church that suggests that faith and money considerations are seasonal and related to the raising of the budget. Third, they may even have been told in some churches that they should not worry about money because the members would take care of that.

In the last ten years, more research and writing on the subject of faith and money has been provided than ever before. Pastors should actively seek to be equipped in this vital area of ministry. They need to recognize that preaching and teaching about faith and money has little to do with budget support. But the connection between faith and money has everything to do with who we serve, what we believe, and how we express our beliefs. Lifestyle is an issue of discipleship, so culling money from that consideration is dysfunctional. Research indicates that money is a major source of stress on individuals and families. The pastor has the forum for addressing this with words of encouragement and direction from Scripture. The idea of the annual stewardship sermon ought to be revised into an intentional plan for addressing various facets of faith and money including personal money management, the challenges of living in a consumer culture, the passionate priorities of life and leisure, wise investment strategies with social consciousness, training our children in life values apart from the marketplace, and effective charitable consideration.

In the last fifty years, the tradition has been that the pastor should not know what people give. This information must be guarded as highly confidential, and the pastor cannot be trusted with the information. The expressed fear has been that the pastor would treat people differently if their financial contributions were known. Of course, the pastor can handle the confidential nature of marriage counseling, moral failure, spiritual crisis, and emotional dilemma, but knowing what people give is just too risky. The presupposition here is that giving is not a spiritual issue. If the pastor has a role in identifying and recruiting leaders, how does the pastor identify people with the gift of giving who could lead on a finance committee if the pastor does not know the members' attitudes about giving?

The pastor should not apologize for addressing faith and money regularly in sermons, prayer, teaching, and conversation. Fear and the desire to protect church members do little to help the members grow or the cause of Christ to flourish. The pastor is in a key role to effect positive change in the area of faith and money and to make the necessary connection between the two. It is common to find a church that seldom meets its mission obligations until a pastoral change takes place. It has little to do with available resources and everything to do with leadership and clear expectations.

The Treasurer

Another leadership role that is fraught with difficulty is that of treasurer. In some churches, the treasurer is a volunteer who stays in the position for years and years. Recently, in a rather large church, the people pointed to the treasurer's twenty-two years of service as commendable. Despite a large number of new people with gifts in the area of administration, this seventy-five-year-old had no intention of ever giving up the position. The church's trust had been damaged by some difficulties in financial decisions, and some changes were happening that had to be addressed; however, no one dared suggest that a change of leadership would be helpful.

It is also a real problem when a treasurer acts as if the money being handled is his or her personal funds and not the church's. Making unilateral final decisions about financial matters is not the job of one individual but the responsibility of the appropriate committee. The treasurer needs to be enlisted for a specific period of time and trained in the written expectations of the job, including how the treasurer relates to other financial leaders. Rotating this position can avoid significant problems and tap into the talent pool within the church.

Finance Committee Members

The same issues can be found with finance committee members. The central problem that can develop in these committees seems to be the enlistment of people who have gifts of finance but not of stewardship. While it is necessary for one leadership group to have the responsibility of oversight of cash flow and financial policies, the same group seldom has the gift of stewardship education or ministry vision. Most often when the church faces a lean cash flow, the first impulse of financial leaders is to freeze spending or to cut expenses from the budget without consideration of the greater purpose of the church. Unfortunately, the gifts of financial management are not encouraged to be diagnostic where cash flow forecasting could avoid these kinds of decisions. And it is common for the financial management group to be assigned responsibility for raising the money for the budget, although creativity and motivation are seldom gifts associated with the finance committee. Often, the common refrain is to have a low-key approach and to report in ways that are actually detrimental. Financial reporting will be addressed in a separate chapter, but the issue here is matching gifts and tasks. Meeting the budget is not the purpose of the church. When a financial committee communicates that the church is healthy or unhealthy on the basis of weekly or monthly financial needs being met or unmet, there is no room for connecting faith and money as a spiritual issue.

Financial Secretaries

Financial secretaries or bookkeepers also have skills related to financial management that are needed, but expectations of this position are too often disproportionate to giftedness. The financial secretary is a support role, and that person should not recommend who should serve in financial leadership roles in the church or be asked to assist in the church annual campaign. Some churches believe that it is essential that the person who fills this position be a church member, while other churches think that the person must not be a church member. Neither view addresses the real needs. The financial secretary should be hired on the basis of experience and skills brought to the job, not because of church membership. Again, the issue of confidentiality is blown out of proportion when it is used to control the selection of a financial secretary. The church should have established internal controls that protect the church as well as the financial secretary. The church should also have oversight of the activities of this position.

A Financial Leadership Team

The best approach to financial leadership in the church seems to be a diversified group of leaders with gifts related to various tasks. The understanding of financial leadership should be expanded, and the team should be enlarged. The church needs a *finance committee* for the oversight of financial management with financial policies, cash flow analysis, effective reporting, and appropriate auditing. But this group is not the senior or superior committee. It is only one committee with one piece of the financial pie.

The church also needs a *budget development committee,* whose task is to acquire input from various ministry leaders about anticipated costs for fulfilling their ministries and how their programs relate to the attainment of church goals and objectives. This group is responsible for communicating the budget for ministry support to the congregation using a variety of means, such as ministry testimonies, ministry fairs, and appropriate ministry information in a narrative budget. This group works with staff and reports their budget to the finance committee. Those serving in this capacity might include people who have a good understanding of the scope of the church's ministry. A finance committee member might serve on this group.

A different group should be developed for stewardship. This *stewardship committee* would include age-group stewardship education, consumer education, designing and implementing the annual campaign, debt counseling, and coordinating other stewardship endeavors, including spiritual gifts, time commitments, and other holistic considerations of stewardship. These people need to be educators, motivators, sales people, marketing types, public relations people who can communicate, motivate, and inspire the congregation.

A different group should have responsibility for presenting the issues of *planned giving and endowment* to the church. Sometimes the trustees are given this responsibility. This group promotes a wills and bequests program and a memorial gift program and provides information about planned gifts, such as life income gifts. These leaders might be found in related fields, such as development positions, insurance, financial estate planning, law, and banking.

The overarching financial team would include representatives from all of these groups. It would not be just the traditional finance committee, who often see their job as matching income and expenses rather than the completion of ministry objectives.

For Further Study

"Creating a Commonwealth: Leading the Saints," Chapter 5 in *Generous Saints: Congregations Rethinking Ethics and Money,* by James Hudnut-Beumler (Alban Institute, 1998).

"Developing Committed Steward Leaders," Chapter 3 in *Developing a Giving Church,* by Stan Toler and Elmer Towns (Beacon Hill Press, 1999).

"Home Remedies: Troubleshooting for Finance Leaders," Chapter 10 in *Get Well! Stay Well! Prescriptions for a Financially Healthy Congregation,* by Wayne C. Barrett (Discipleship Resources, 1997).

"Leadership for Giving," Chapter 3 in *Don't Shoot the Horse ('Til You Know How to Drive the Tractor): Moving From Annual Fund Raising to a Life of Giving,* by Herb Mather (Discipleship Resources, 1994).

"The Minister's Role in Fund-raising," Chapter 6 in *Creating Congregations of Generous People,* by Michael Durall (Alban Institute, 1999).

"Spiritually Mature Leadership," Chapter 9 in *Growing Givers' Hearts: Treating Fundraising as Ministry,* by Thomas H. Jeavons and Rebekah Burch Basinger (Jossey-Bass, 2000).

"Why Are Pastors Uneasy About Money?" Chapter 1 in *Plain Talk About Churches and Money,* by Dean Hoge, Patrick McNamara, and Charles Zech (Alban Institute, 1998).

Chapter Five

Communication

Making the connection between faith and money is complicated when we use methods that are no longer effective or have a negative tone. Not too long ago in a suburban church, the communication had evolved based on the church's unhappy experiences. When established, the church was in the heart of a growing and developing residential community, but the community had changed over the years from single-family dwellings for middle-income families to a transitional community with multiethnic apartment complexes and commercial development. The church had also suffered through a regular rotation of short-term pastorates. The church's vision had moved from advancing the kingdom of God to survival. The church had made several bad decisions about financial issues, including building to remedy their problems and then finding they could not afford what they built. A visit to their church in September found a dimly lit foyer (with low-wattage lighting to save money), no regular written communication with church members (the church newsletter cancelled to save money), and a dispirited leadership group. It had become hard to get people to serve in leadership responsibilities. Although visitors regularly attended worship services, few joined the church. In the foyer was a series of eight posterboards that gave a financial report for each month of the year. On each was the entry for the monthly budget required, the amount received, and a deficit number recorded in red.

Think about the reason for and effect of this kind of reporting. The purpose was to let the people know, but the effect was the communication of hopelessness and defeat. Visitors were not motivated to join a sinking ship, and members were not encouraged to give more. The entire communication depicted a need that apparently surpassed capacity to give. This kind of reporting is sadly commonplace in many churches.

Common Ineffective Communication Practices

Ineffective communication includes using this kind of systemically negative reporting as well as other mediums of communication that complicate understanding. One example is dividing the annual budget by weekly or monthly increments and communicating weekly and monthly needs. This leads to a constant reporting of negative numbers, since church revenue does not come in equivalent weekly or monthly amounts. Such reporting actually creates a false expectation, since most churches experience a disproportionate fourth quarter. Knowingly reporting finances in such an arbitrary manner does not encourage or give a meaningful point of accurate comparison.

Another poor communication and analysis tool is using the term *giving unit.* One family might have several givers, and that would skew any meaningful communication or analysis. The economic unit of meaning in our culture is the family unit. Reporting and analyzing by households instead of individuals would be a step in the right direction.

Another poor communication approach is to use a line-item budget as a primary tool to communicate the church finances to the members. Line items might make a lot of sense to the finance committee of accountants, bankers, or financial types, but a line-item budget seldom helps the average church member develop a clear understanding of what is happening or the effect of giving. These poor methods can be complicated even further by using other 1950's modes of communication, such as a thermometer to indicate levels of success. Many people under fifty years of age may have never seen a thermometer, except for a digital one. Why do we use such outdated approaches?

Effective Methods of Communication

A more effective reporting style would be to re-evaluate how and what we communicate. The use of a narrative budget instead of a line-item budget is a dramatically more effective approach. (The narrative budget will be explained in detail in Chapter Seven.)

Weekly and monthly comparisons are irrelevant because of holidays, five-Sunday months, weather anomalies, and program priorities. The basic communication that would provide more meaningful information is a monthly statement of income and expenses without any reference to the budget and then a more complete quarterly faith and finance report. This quarterly report should include several kinds of information.

- Quarterly summaries of income and expenses ought to be communicated. Then these income and expense categories ought to be compared with the same quarters last year and with averages of the same quarter over the last three to five years. The quarterly report also ought to include ministry reports connecting funding and ministry accomplishments.
- The quarterly report can include continued stewardship education with mini-lessons, cartoons, and written statements of support. Think how different this report would be to that suburban church that was mired in communicating hopelessness (page 33).
- Effective reporting would also include the development and communication of financial policies governing annual, capital, and deferred giving. Designated giving, cash management, and reserve investment returns might also be included in these policies. Gift acceptance policies can not only provide an effective communication on how financial issues are managed by the church but also help prevent problems when inappropriate designations are requested or complicated in-kind gifts, such as supplies, equipment, or professional services, become issues.

Express Appreciation

One other kind of communication that enhances giving in a church is expressing appreciation for gifts. The church should model gratitude. However, while most nonprofit agencies express thanks for gifts, only a few churches have gone to that effort. While each church has its own culture about how to say thank you, some ideas include

- personal hand-written thank-you notes;
- pastoral luncheons or coffees;
- volunteer appreciation gatherings;
- recognition in the newsletter or bulletin or on the website;
- verbal expressions of appreciation, such as "great job," "thank you," or "good work";
- small appreciation gifts, such as bookmarks or movie tickets;
- bulletin board thank-yous
- birthday cards or calls

Appreciation can be expressed in many ways. The method you choose should be tasteful and in keeping with the spiritual tone of the church.

While some might fear expressing appreciation, this hesitation is usually rooted in exposing confidential donor information or upsetting non-donors. With regard to the former, sensitive donor information need not be sacrificed to express appreciation. With regard to upsetting those who do not give, remember that you cannot lose what you do not have. Affirm the positive habits of the congregation in appropriate ways.

Communicate Openly and Frequently

A final observation about communication is that it should be open and frequent. Discussing the issue of faith and money in individual relationships, in covenant groups, in formal and informal teaching opportunities, in pastoral counseling, and from the pulpit on Sunday should not be only during the budget-raising campaign. We cannot expect to grow in this area by addressing it annually and discussing it hesitantly. If the way we have communicated in the past has led us to where we are today in faith and money, does it make sense to continue the same kind of limited and erroneous communication that will yield the same results?

For Further Study

At Ease: Discussing Money and Values in Small Groups, by John and Sylvia Ronsvalle (Alban Institute, 1998).

Creating a Climate for Giving, by Donald W. Joiner (Discipleship Resources, 2001).

Developing a Giving Church, by Stan Toler and Elmer Towns (Beacon Hill Press, 1999).

"Telling Stories," Chapter 8 in *Don't Shoot the Horse ('Til You Know How to Drive the Tractor): Moving From Annual Fund Raising to a Life of Giving,* by Herb Mather (Discipleship Resources, 1994).

Chapter Six

Education

Money is one of the yardsticks by which we measure our personal success in today's society. It defines us, in part. It empowers independence, status, and position. Society and business clearly understand how to use mass media to instill hope for the attainment of personal goals and to sell products that promise fulfillment. Is there something to be learned by the church with regard to getting across its message of faith and money?

Demanding Ministries, Declining Resources

Many pastors in growing congregations, especially those with younger families, experience the goods and services of the church being consumed each week. How does the church bridge the gap between demanding ministries and declining resources?

- First, we must get beyond thinking of stewardship as an event to be addressed when there is a problem.
- Second, we must use our creative intelligence to address stewardship education in comprehensive, consistent, ongoing ways.

We will never have enough gimmicks to secure adequate financial resources for ministry, apart from spiritually educating people about faith and money. In order to excel in the grace and understanding of faith and money, stewardship must become a higher priority, both in the classroom and in the pew.

Problematic Attitudes

The painful truth is that the church has failed to teach stewardship as a vital principle for Christian discipleship. It has not connected stewardship with Bible study, missions, or other aspects of ministry. For example, you seldom see a long-term study on stewardship listed as a study option for small groups in church. In most cases, stewardship education is secondary to everything else. Too frequently, stewardship education consists of a frantic report from the finance committee on how far off track the church is with regard to expected income. Then church leaders attempt to draft a compelling letter that harkens back to Scriptures to motivate members to give. This sort of bandage approach will never move the people to new habits of sustained faithful giving.

Let's begin by identifying a couple of problematic attitudes.

- The *gatekeeper attitude* is often characterized as follows: "We cannot support missions or other Christian outreach causes, because we need every penny to pay the bills of our new church." Often, clergy are the main carriers of this message. Many clergy have readily placed themselves in a gatekeeper position. When a church cannot see beyond its own local bill-paying agenda, it models this attitude to the members. As a result, how can the church expect members to see beyond their own personal needs? A selfish church is a shrinking church.

- Only the *entitlement attitude* surpasses the gatekeeper attitude. This attitude is self-centered, insidious, and counterproductive to the cause of Christ. It can be characterized as follows: "This is our church. We paid for the facilities, and we will not allow kids from the neighborhood to tear the place up. Close down the day school so that we can keep our facilities like new. Let the kids go elsewhere. We cannot be all things to all people."

Both of these unbiblical attitudes can be reshaped by positive stewardship education.

Effective Stewardship Education

Experts in communication say that, in order to fully get the message, people need to be exposed to the same information in at least five different ways for a minimum of five to seven times. In today's information society, there is significant competition for our attention. The church exists in the same society; therefore, it is incumbent upon the church to educate the congregation about the ministry and business of the church and God's expectations of us.

Stewardship education must be an intentional effort to address the challenges we face, to build a theological foundation, and to provide clear biblical instruction that leads to some basic principles about faith and money. Each age group in the church has its own particular needs and educational approaches. The priorities of stewardship education should target the points of need and resistance. Once this is done, the church can effectively tailor educational tools and venues for all age groups.

Additionally, the church would do well to target the emphasis. For example, ask and answer the question, What are the primary needs as they relate to stewardship education within our adult classes, in our worship experience, or among our senior adults, children, and youth? In some cases, you may find that a primary need in the children's area is to teach basic concepts of commitment. Further evaluating the actual giving patterns of middle-aged adults may reveal a need to emphasize the tithe as a basic cornerstone of commitment perspective.

Adults

Adult groups often pose significant challenges for stewardship education, since life situations are varied and old non-giving habits are hard to reshape. We assume too much if we believe that members automatically make the connection between faith and money, apart from biblical teachings on the subject. Concerted efforts to understand and embrace the connection between faith and money must focus on whom we serve as Christians, rather than on our church's need for money. The focus must be on faith and responsible use of the resources that have been entrusted to us. Ultimately, we must be enriched in our understanding that our lives are not about our plans, our careers, our finances, our vacations, our families, and our health. Life is about God. Our desire to please God must overshadow our personal desire for ownership and control of our resources. The educational focus must be about faith.

Stewardship education can help to refocus daily concerns toward faith-based decisions and practical ways to give that may result in improvement of one's life situations. Let people know about various ways to give. Most members seldom think beyond writing a check, never considering other possible creative ways to give. A worthy goal of stewardship education will make members aware that by giving appreciated assets, for example, they may avoid costly capital gains tax and receive the full tax benefit of charitable contributions. The church can then convert such gifts to cash and apply them as needed or stipulated by the donor. The more the church educates members about giving, the greater the available support for ministry. While in some cases the church may suggest that the donor dispose of the asset and give the proceeds, a priority should be to make it easy for people to find ways in which they can advance the cause of Christ through wise management of all resources. Make stewardship a regular part of the church newsletter, instead of a space filler.

Effective stewardship education should target the demographics of the church. For example, senior adults may feel as though their changing life situations no longer allow them to be financially supportive of God's work to the same degree that they have been. They may also be concerned about what the future holds. Through encouraging stewardship education and planned gifts, the senior adults in the church can find various ways to give, some of which may improve their day-to-day life situation and, in the end, help the church's ministries beyond what they can imagine.

Children and Youth

Each of us recognizes the importance of children and youth in our churches. We readily step out in faith to provide adequate space for these two areas of ministry. We work to involve children and youth in every appropriate aspect of the church's ministry, from prayer to worship; yet we do little to teach faith and money. It is never too early to begin teaching responsible stewardship and commitment. If we wait until our children and youth reach adulthood, we will continue to be behind the educational curve. We all tend to think of children and youth as the church of tomorrow. Indeed, they are the church of today, though our intent to teach them about the connection between faith and money may well determine the church's ability to fulfill its mission in the future.

Whether children, youth, or adult, stewardship education must be embraced by church leaders, rather than simply being suggested by the finance committee. Imagine what the next generation of church leaders will be able to accomplish if lessons on stewardship become as commonplace in today's Sunday school as those on Noah and the ark.

A Vital Spiritual Process

In the final analysis, laity and clergy must embrace stewardship education as a vital spiritual process, rather than as a seasonal event. Those who are charged with the educational responsibility must be trained and prepared to teach and mentor others. The church's commitment to excel in the area of stewardship education must be backed with an action plan, goals, tasks, and timetables. By establishing benchmarks and ways to measure the outcome, the church can reach its stewardship educational objectives. In the end, people will learn that the first and foremost principle of stewardship is that God owns it all. They will be enriched and, in turn, will enrich the ministries of the church through their faithful, sacrificial goals. Educational efforts must be consistent and varied to be effective.

The Bible must be the basis for the teaching. Without this scriptural basis, lessons will seldom be life changing or enduring. Prayer must be an intentional, abiding framework. Crisis communication to address a financial shortfall is not education. Simply addressing stewardship once a year, if at all, is not enough. Demonstration of our stewardship is not how much we give but how we react when there is not enough to give.

Recently, a pastor told about a man in the congregation who took great pride in pointing out that God had been faithful to him despite his lack of support of the church. His crops were larger than ever before, and his seven-day work week had paid richly. The pastor pointed out to the man that not all of God's accounts are settled at the end of the month or harvest season. God's plan is unfolding. Get comfortable with the fact that you will never know the future but that God does. Embrace the importance of year-round, life-changing stewardship education.

> They are to do good, to be rich in good works, generous, and ready to share, thus storing up for themselves the treasure of a good foundation for the future, so that they may take hold of the life that really is life.   (1 Timothy 6:18-19)

For Further Study

Afire With God: Spirit-ed Stewardship for a New Century, by Betsy Schwarzentraub (Discipleship Resources, 2000).

Holy Smoke! Whatever Happened to Tithing? by J. Clif Christopher and Herb Mather (Discipleship Resources, 1999).

Money Isn't/Is Everything: What Jesus Said About the Spiritual Power of Money, by Herb Miller (Discipleship Resources, 1994).

That's What My Mother Taught Me (and Other Ways Generous Givers Develop), by Herb Mather (Discipleship Resources, 2001).

Chapter Seven

The Church Budget

The church budget can be considered in more than one way, depending on the stewardship culture of the congregation. Ideally, the church budget is an expression of a church's commitment to its mission. It is a *ministry action plan* for what the congregation believes God has called it to do. In preparing the budget, church leaders (and the congregation) can define their vision and state how they will carry out ministry. A church budget can declare: "This is who we are as the people of God."

In other instances, the church budget may be the official document by which a congregation places God on notice concerning the limitations the church plans to put on God's grace in the coming year. The culture being communicated in this second perspective is that the church is "making its budget," with little consideration of ministry accomplishment. However, the church budget was never intended to be such an absolute, intransigent document.

Budgeting: A Changing Process

Until the mid-twentieth century, budget planning was simple for businesses, family life, and the church. In rural, village, and city churches, stewards received people's offerings and faithfully managed them. Limited cash offerings, as well as gifts of farm products and other merchandise, paid the preacher and provided for simple church needs. When special needs arose, the people collected an offering of cash and/or materials. "The Lord's Acre" stewardship projects, special offerings, fundraising projects, and even the renting of pews provided additional funds for ministry as physical and ministry needs occurred.

Giving of cash increased as churches grew larger and more people received salaries. Wise and responsible church leaders developed a church budget to administer funds, usually following simple business models. Line-item budgets enabled the church to manage spending. Furthermore, budgets provided a way to report to the congregation, and that gave people confidence in how funds were being spent.

Today, the church does business in a culture that demands greater accountability, so church leaders cannot ignore accountable stewardship. Diminishing trust of all institutions, including the local church, means that people want to know what the church is doing with the money they give. Today, people are willing to give when they believe their giving is making a difference.

People who give insist on participating in how the funds are spent. Of course, the entire congregation does not become the finance committee. But planning allows ministry leaders and selected members of the congregation an opportunity to represent the congregation in budget development.

The Budget: A Living Document

The work of budget development is strengthened by church members who understand the church's vision for ministry and have a passion for doing it. The process of budget development is stewardship of financial resources entrusted by the congregation to those who plan the budget. This planning is not about money, though; it is about growing in Christ, as individual believers and as a congregation. It is about ministry to the congregation, the community, and the world. The budget must empower the church's vision for ministry.

The purpose of the budget is to develop a financial plan for ministry for a calendar or fiscal year. However, developing this document is not the end of the process. It is the beginning, a significant first step. An effective budget estimates income and spending for a specific time period, usually one year.

A church budget should be a dynamic document, as alive as the congregation's vision, ministry, and growth. As ministry needs and giving change, the budget must change. To some leaders and church members, this concept of a changing budget rather than a fixed budget is a new concept.

With the fixed approach, the budget becomes a sterile method for controlling program and ministry activities and presumes that the challenges and opportunities God reveals do not change with the passage of time.

In the business world, growing companies often change their spending plans as products and markets change. A church should not be afraid to make changes (if not month to month, at least annually). If giving decreases, review spending priorities. Give funds to activities that most effectively enable the congregation to carry out ministry and energize growth. When income increases, review the budget and commit new resources to ministries and programs previously underfunded or not funded at all. Nothing requires that decisions made in budget planning cannot change as needs and circumstances change.

Whether you are developing a church budget for the first time or designing a new approach for your budgeting process, keep in mind that a budget

- enables the church to be responsible and responsive in funding ministries;
- creates openness for a growing vision;
- involves members in budget development;
- defines priorities in planning ministry;
- communicates to the congregation the need for financial stewardship;
- builds up the congregation's confidence and trust in church leaders;
- provides an effective tool for stewardship education.

The Budget Development Committee

The budget development committee consists of three or four people of vision appointed from the committee on finance. These people will work with the senior pastor, the church council or board chairperson, and the lay leader. Ministry chairpersons should not be on this committee, since their job is to work with their ministry teams to determine the ministry needs of the individual ministry budgets.

The budget development committee has four primary objectives:
- gather information via budget request forms (see the sample on page 51);
- interview representatives of each ministry expense center (any ministry area incurring expenses supported by the budget);
- process the requests and proposals of the different expense centers;
- develop a proposed budget for the church.

Once the proposed budget is developed, the committee presents it to the finance committee for discussion and consideration. The budget development committee must be prepared to attend the church council or board meeting to answer questions. Then the budget development committee should help the stewardship ministry team write the line-item budget in a narrative form for distribution to the congregation and/or use during the annual stewardship campaign. (See pages 49–50 for help in understanding why a narrative budget is important and guidelines for writing a narrative budget.) The budget development committee should also seek the counsel of the senior pastor, the lay leader, and other appropriate congregational leaders to decide the most effective ways to communicate the budget to the entire congregation. They must be creative in finding ways to distribute the narrative budget. When budget revisions are needed, the budget development committee should spearhead these activities, since the insight they gleaned from the total process will be beneficial.

The entire budget development schedule will require about eleven weeks, from the point of appointing the budget development committee until the final adoption by the church council. (The flow chart on pages 47–48 can help the committee keep track of the progress of their assigned work.)

For Further Study

"The Narrative Budget," Appendix 1 in *Revolutionizing Christian Stewardship for the 21st Century: Lessons From Copernicus,* by Dan R. Dick (Discipleship Resources, 1997).

Step 1: Appoint a Budget Development Committee
(11 Weeks Before the Presentation of the Budget)

- The committee is three or four people from the committee on finance, along with the senior pastor, the chairperson of the church council or board, and the church lay leader.
- The committee will need information about current church ministries and budgets so that they can begin a preliminary budget outline.

Step 2: Committee Meets for the First Time
(10 Weeks Before the Presentation of the Budget)

- The committee
  — elects its chairperson;
  — reviews the objectives and goals of their work;
  — sets a timeline for the budget development process;
  — sets guidelines for budget requests, without limiting vision for ministry;
  — selects the person who will explain the process to the ministry leaders.

Step 3: Committee Meets With Ministry Team Leaders
(9 Weeks Before the Presentation of the Budget)

- The committee reviews the budget development process and timeline with ministry team leaders.
- Ministry team leaders receive budget request forms, along with a deadline for completion of the requests.

Step 4: Ministry Leaders Review Their Ministries
(2- to 3-week period, until request forms are due)

- Committee members talk with ministry leaders individually to review the process and to answer questions, as needed.
- The ministry leaders work with their ministry teams on the financial needs to fulfill their ministry during the next year. They will ask:
  — What are the primary needs of our congregation?
  — What did we do this year? Was it effective?
  — How can we improve our ministry area?
  — Are there areas to be phased out from last year's ministry activity?
  — What new endeavors need consideration for funding?
  — What is our proposed budget to meet next year's ministry plan?
- Each ministry group prepares a budget request form. (See the sample form on page 51.)

Step 5: Committee Evaluates the Budget Request Forms
(5 Weeks Before the Presentation of the Budget)
- As the committee reviews the budget request forms, they will ask:
  — Do the proposed ministry plans contribute to the accomplishment of the church's mission and vision?
  — Does any part of the request need clarification? (If so, the development committee will contact the ministry leader for additional information.)
- The committee prepares a line-item budget and makes plans for preparing a narrative budget.

Step 6: Committee Presents the Proposed Line-Item Budget to the Committee on Finance
(3 Weeks Before the Presentation of the Budget)
- The committee invites ministry leaders, as needed, to attend the meeting to answer questions about budget requests.
- The committee receives suggestions and makes changes, as needed.

Step 7: Committee Prepares a Narrative Budget
(1 Week Before the Presentation of the Budget)
- The committee completes work on revisions of the line-item budget.
- The narrative budget is prepared by a small subgroup that includes committee members, staff, and a creative writer. (See "Building a Narrative Budget," on pages 49–50, for a description of a narrative budget.)

Step 8: Committee Presents the Line-Item Budget and the Narrative Budget to the Church Council or Board
(The Week of the Presentation of the Budget)
- The committee presents the budgets and answers questions, as needed.
- If the budgets are approved, the committee moves on to Step 9.
- If the council or board requests changes, the committee continues its work.

Step 9: Committee Communicates Ministry Plans
(After the Budget Is Adopted)
- The budget development committee may
  — develop a communication piece to inform the church of the ministry plans to be accomplished during the new budget year;
  — use the narrative budget and the communication piece as parts of the annual financial campaign;
  — identify and use creative ways to say thank you to those who made commitments or estimates of giving;
  — plan and implement a year-round emphasis on stewardship education.

What Is a Narrative Budget?

A narrative budget is a representation of the line-item budget in simple, easy-to-read, descriptive terms. It transforms a line-item listing of money and expenses into an exciting and enlivening picture of ministries and missional expressions of the congregation.

Why Use a Narrative Budget?

Research studies indicate that churches often fail to communicate the value of the ministries they provide. People who give are not always aware of the changes occurring in personal lives through the ministries of their church. Therefore, contributors have a limited understanding of the use of their gifts or the relationships with those who receive the ministry benefits.

Although a line-item budget is an effective tool for the committee on finance to manage financial resources, it is not an effective means for interpreting ministries or their impact on people's lives. On the other hand, the narrative budget helps members of the congregation understand what the church is doing in ministry, evangelism, discipleship training, benevolences, and missions. It is a connecting link between the contributor and the church's ministries. A well-composed narrative budget will educate and inspire everyone.

Where Do We Start?

Enlist a small committee composed of representatives from the finance, budget development, and/or stewardship committees; the church staff; and a skilled writer and graphic artist to create the narrative budget. The committee will do the following:

1. Review the line-item budget and group budget items by ministry areas, such as worship, education, youth, missions.
2. Review the congregation's mission statement and creatively describe the various ministries of the congregation as they fulfill the mission statement.
3. Consider prorating all salaries, building costs, operational expenses, and overhead expenses as well as program funds into specific ministry areas.
4. Write one or two descriptive paragraphs for each ministry area. Use examples that enable readers to understand the impact the ministries have in changing lives. Use stories to illustrate the ministry's effectiveness during the previous and current years. Picture new or expanded ministry needs as the rationale for increased funding.

5. Provide a positive, clear explanation of significant funding changes, whether they are proposed increases or decreases.
6. Expand the reader's horizons by identifying several relevant and exciting additional or future ministries that could be undertaken with funding beyond the budgetary financial projections.
7. Consider a pie chart that uses ministry areas to depict the budget visually.
8. Prepare the narrative budget in an attractive, inviting, readable brochure format.
9. Determine ways to use the narrative budget most effectively to communicate the exciting message of ministry throughout the congregation.

Budget Request Form
for _____ (*Year*)

Ministry Expense Center: _____

Contact Person: _____ Phone: _____

1. Describe your proposed plan for next year, stating how it relates to the church's vision and mission statements.

_____
_____
_____
_____

2. What changes are planned to improve this ministry for next year?

_____
_____
_____
_____

3. Estimate the cost for each ministry event or expense item.

_____
_____
_____
_____

4. Estimate monthly expenditures.   Total Amount Requested: _____

January	_____	May	_____	September	_____
February	_____	June	_____	October	_____
March	_____	July	_____	November	_____
April	_____	August	_____	December	_____

5. Do you have dream plans if additional funds are available? Briefly describe the dreams, with an estimate of both the amount and timing of funding that will be needed.

_____
_____
_____
_____

Chapter Eight

Approaches That Have Never Worked

O ver the years, there have been many annual stewardship approaches that seemed to be self-perpetuating, some that have outlived their effectiveness, and others that have never worked. By bringing some of these approaches to the forefront, we hope to inspire discernment of stewardship approaches that may be considered and to encourage the use of those that are spiritually rooted, time tested, and proven successful. A common fundamental axiom is that people need to give more than the church needs the money. Here are some approaches that have never worked.

1. Increase the Budget, But Don't Plan to Fund Expenditures

Budget planning that does not include how expenditures may be funded makes little sense. A "whatever happens, happens" operating plan holds little hope that the church will be able to reach its ministry goals. The church is a business, God's business. Does it not follow that we should do our best to tell the story and inspire people to want to be a part of God's work through the church? Every solid business plan includes advertising and marketing to tell the story and promote participation. Solid methods and procedures that inform, inspire, call the people to prayer, and ask the people to participate are mandatory. When left on their own, too many people seek the lowest possible level of participation—if they participate at all. If meeting ministry needs is important to the church, a specific plan of action is required.

2. Deliver Materials, But Avoid Personal Contact

A lot of motion is involved in delivering to people's homes a packet of materials needed to make a pledge. This approach is short on inspiration, long on effort, and limited in the area of education about planned, visionary ministries. It is labor intensive and does not use personal contact that would involve the people in understanding and participating in the ministries of the church. In fact, delivering materials, rather than conveying the story, becomes the most important thing.

3. Cloak of Secrecy/No Commitment Card

This approach calls for a church member to sign a card indicating his or her intent to give and then to seal the envelope and never look at it again. Sometimes, these cards are somehow made holy or are consecrated by being stored in a box under the pulpit or altar. In some situations, the person may get the card back at the end of the year to see how personal giving has measured up to expectations. The secrecy aspect of this approach is supposed to have some superior spiritual dimension. From whom is the secret of giving being kept? God already knows our hearts.

> When you give alms, do not let your left hand know what your right hand is doing, so that your alms may be done in secret; and your Father who sees in secret will reward you.
>
> (Matthew 6:3-4)

Some have concluded from this text that acceptable giving must be secret, that no one should know how much we give; thus, signing a commitment card is wrong. However, the context of this passage shows that Jesus was condemning the display that the Pharisees made of religion.

How do we reconcile this secret giving with the fact that, on the last week of Jesus' brief time on earth, Jesus stood in the Temple treasury watching what people gave? Using Matthew 6:3-4 as a reason not to sign a commitment card or to do so in secret seems inconsistent, especially considering our readiness to itemize our gifts on an income tax return form when we think we will get some direct personal benefit.

The secrecy approach has other serious problems associated with it. For example, without knowledge of what people plan to give, the church is hard pressed to commit to ministries that perhaps cannot occur. When members sign commitment cards, they indicate a willingness to be a part of the financial support of ministries, in cooperation with church leaders. With knowledge of potential income, solid planning for ministries can take place. The Scriptures make clear that giving is vital to one's spiritual growth. Developing healthy, God-honoring attitudes about giving must be a church priority. Secret giving is fearful giving.

4. Fair Share

This approach has many problems. First, not everyone in the church will participate in giving. Unfortunately, the church has not yet achieved that high spiritual standard of participation. Next, if everyone were asked to give a fair share, some people would be robbed of a huge blessing and the joy of deciding for themselves to give out of the store of what God has entrusted to them. Other people may be hard pressed to give up to the average. Many of the concepts of giving that Jesus taught are contrary to everyday thought: "How can I repay the LORD for all his goodness to me?" (Psalm 116:12, NIV). God is no doubt interested in how we will answer that question. Thank God there is no such thing as a fair share of grace. Though the Scriptures clearly outline God's expectations, giving is an individual spiritual matter.

5. Adoption

In this approach, certain items are extracted from the church budget and special fundraisers are held to underwrite them. However, for the long-term health and well-being of the congregation, it is best to present the entire ministry plans for the coming year and identify the resources that are needed to fund them. People appreciate having all of this information in one place, so the church should not nickel and dime people to the point of irritation throughout the year. Members tend to remember how frequently they are asked to give more than the amount they gave when asked to fund the ministry budget. In addition, the adoption approach invites competition among various ministry groups by shifting the focus of the church's overall missional objectives to pet projects. Those projects that have strong advocates receive funding, while other worthy ministries may suffer or be discontinued because of lack of funding.

6. Annual and Capital Campaign Combined

The Scriptures refer to two types of gifts: those that *run* the temple and those that *build* the temple. Both capital initiatives and annual budget appeals offer two dynamic opportunities for teaching what the Bible has to say about giving. Often, church members say that it is confusing when the church combines capital and annual appeals. This approach encourages members to think in terms of one gift, suggesting that the church split it as desired. Combining these two approaches does little to focus on stewardship growth. When the two appeals are combined, both are diminished.

7. Scaring People Into Giving/Fear Tactic

This method is contrary to what the Bible has to say about giving, although God surely has expectations of us to give. Giving should be an act of worship, an expression of our thanks for God's indescribable gift to us. When people are pressured or shamed into giving, they look for every opportunity or excuse not to live up to the commitment they have made. The spiritual stature of a person is not revealed by his or her ability to make money but by how the person uses money. The church should teach the biblical basis for giving and, in so doing, create a desire for faithful giving. Consider David's motive for giving: "Because of my devotion to the house of my God I give" (1 Chronicles 29:3). When the church emphasizes shame and fear as motivations for giving, it undercuts the whole of the biblical principle of giving.

8. Confirming Poor Habits

From time to time, churches unknowingly confirm the giving lethargy and poor habits of members. One way they do this is by using the stairstep chart, a graphic that shows the number of families within the church that fall into various giving groups. Members say that when they see that they are among the top givers to the church, they are shocked. Based on their own giving, these members think many families should be giving more than they do. They then go on to say, "Well, I must not be doing so badly after all." Other members locate themselves at the bottom rung of the stair, in the company of many more people giving at the lower level. They say, "Well, I know I could do better. But, look, my giving is not so bad. After all, several more people in the church give as I do." Church leaders planning communication tools for encouraging and promoting faithful giving should carefully evaluate each idea, asking whether each tool or communication method encourages faithfulness in giving or confirms poor giving habits already in existence. "How can I repay the LORD for all his goodness to me?" (Psalm 116:12, NIV).

9. The Church Needs Money/ Failure to Connect Money to Mission

The fact that the church needs operating money has little appeal and hardly inspires giving. A poll of the congregation would no doubt confirm that most families want more operating money in their household accounts. When the church uses money instead of mission as an approach, it puts the church in competition with prior claim. Prior claim says, "My personal possessions and resources are continually under siege by demands of the government." The church is then added to an ever-growing list of entities, including other worthy nonprofit organizations, that are attempting to take away personal resources. Few institutional givers support the church generously out of duty or because they ought to. Most people would agree that the church should survive, but few would consider it primary that the church thrive financially. However, when the church presents giving as an expression of our love of God, an act of faithful discipleship, it sets into motion a desire to give. When the church presents life-changing ministries that can capture the hearts of the people, giving is inspired.

10. The Ship Is Sinking

When was the last time you phoned your broker and requested that he or she purchase one thousand shares of the worst-performing stock? Aside from the spiritual motivation, people want to give to winning causes. The cry-wolf approach has a short shelf life. The ship-is-sinking approach is rarely perceived as related to the stingy giving habits or poor stewardship response of the congregation. Instead, people become suspicious of the day-to-day management of funds. After all, couldn't those in management do a better job and avoid this? Missing from this approach is biblical teaching on stewardship and inspiration for giving. The church is the bride of Christ. Presenting the church as a beggar or a victim erodes confidence and sends mixed signals. The overriding message seems to be that if no one else is responding, why should I?

11. Give and Trust Us to Use It Wisely

The church should model ethics and accountability. Few of us would contribute to an organization without confidence that the gift would help accomplish the goals of the organization. We expect accountability. Organizations and agencies have been set up to monitor and instill donor confidence. However, we hear many horror stories of embezzlement, misuse of funds, and corruption in the church, just as in other organizations. Church leaders must model wise stewardship and prudent management to encourage people to believe in their trustworthiness. Routine reports throughout the year of funds received and the use of tithes and offerings encourage giving.

12. We Don't Talk About Money From the Pulpit

When clergy ascribe to this insidious approach, it can become embedded in the church's DNA in a surprisingly short period. It should be no surprise that giving to support ministry is low when laity and clergy portray attitudes about annual stewardship that can be described as "less is best" or "how little can we do and get by?" Those working with stewardship may unknowingly send the negative message that stewardship is a dreadful responsibility. No wonder it is difficult to get people to serve on finance committees or in stewardship planning and education. It is the church's responsibility to develop within the congregation a strong sense of God's ownership and our stewardship of possessions. The message from the pulpit should advocate and support this biblical principle. If clergy used Jesus' model in teaching possessions and giving as keys to the Kingdom, seventeen sermons per year would be on stewardship, rather than the usual one to four. Church leaders find it hard to inspire giving when they do not practice and model it. The cardinal rule of stewardship is that leaders give first.

13. Holistic Stewardship

This cafeteria-style approach encourages members to choose from an array of entrees, including time, presence, prayers, service, and money. While we should be encouraged to become whole stewards, the holistic stewardship message is garbled and misshaped to fit the comfort level of those presenting it. The biblical message gets lost in the shuffle, and the appeal becomes skewed: If you cannot give money, then surely you can give some time or maybe a few prayers in lieu of your financial resources. Churches sometimes go as far as to say: "We realize that some people may not be able to give, so do something you know you can do, such as supporting the church with your prayers, presence, or perhaps service."

14. Blue Ribbon Panel

From time to time, a church forms an elite small group responsible for putting together the stewardship emphasis. This group retains ownership of the process and fails to involve others. However, the more people involved in promoting good stewardship, the better. When people are involved, it becomes an educational and spiritual process for those involved and builds ownership and understanding for the entire congregation. Involvement equips others to tell the story and mentors members into leadership roles. It spreads the blessings.

15. Failure to Communicate the Cause and Effect

This approach is similar to the church-needs-money approach already mentioned. When the church fails to let members know that their giving sets off the chain reaction of meeting sincere needs, pleasing God, and engendering blessings, it misses opportunities to disciple people in the grace of giving. Take every opportunity to communicate the results of giving, both for the individual and for the church's ability to minister.

16. Leave Us Alone and We Will Come Home

This approach is often reflective of fear that the members do not like to be asked to give or that they will get angry at being asked to give. Church leaders sometimes say that they are afraid that members will leave and go to another church. This fear grows into an enduring resistance to educate the congregation on stewardship matters or to ask people to give. When church leaders give into this fear, they probably do not ascribe to the biblical basis for stewardship themselves.

Fundamentally, we invest a major part of our lives accumulating resources. According to Scripture, God identifies us as wise or foolish based on how we use our resources. Without a challenge, most of us seek our own personal low levels of giving.

17. Apologetic

This approach, which is popular with many clergy and church leaders, begins with an apology for asking people to give: "Now we come to that dreaded time in the service when we take up the offering. I do not really like to preach about money, but I was told by our church leaders that I had to do it. Please bear with me and I will be as brief as possible." But remember, faithful, biblically-based stewardship is empowering, so it needs no apology.

18. Denominational

Some church members readily point to different denominations or congregations and attribute their superior giving habits as intrinsic to the denomination. Somewhere along the way, perhaps some denominations raised the teaching of biblically-based stewardship as a priority. From the standpoint of meeting denominational needs, sometimes people expect denominational loyalty to be enough to inspire giving to support a denomination's ministries. This is simply not the case. Some church members continue to be suspicious of the governmental nature of the hierarchy and the wise use of funds. Some describe the denomination as taxation without proper representation, because they do not agree with the denomination's stance on certain social or moral issues. When it comes to asking for gifts above what constituent congregations may already be giving or paying, the denomination, like the local congregation, must connect money and mission.

While stewardship benefits from fresh new approaches, people ultimately must be put in touch with the mission of the church. Beyond this, they must be called to action or asked to give. We seldom use the word *forever* as it relates to earthly things, as we can hardly comprehend eternity. We need to know, though, that when we give, we can give to eternal things. Talk openly about financial stewardship in ways that educate and inspire people. Talk less about money and more about mission and ministries that make a difference in the lives of people. Understand that you can take it with you, in the form of the souls who have found the way, in part due to your faithful gifts to support the work of your church. Recently, a man told me that the more money he gave to the church, the more his company prospered. It seems to be consistently true among those who give that we cannot outgive God.

For Further Study

Generous People: How to Encourage Vital Stewardship, by Eugene Grimm (Abingdon Press, 1992).

Chapter Nine
How to Think

When it comes to faith and money, we need to think better. Clergy and lay leaders have joked for years about the attitude reflected by the phrase "we've never done it that way before." Nowhere is that more tragic than in this area of spiritual life. The idea that we must not change oral tradition and cultural momentum even though it no longer serves the church effectively seems to be entrenched in the minds of many leaders. This attitude might be understandable if our results were better. However, with the decline of membership and loyalty in denominational life and with the changing values and perspectives of new generations, continuing to think about faith and money with a Depression-era mentality adversely affects the mission of the church and the maturity of the saints.

Old Ways of Thinking

Institutional loyalty can no longer be assumed as a cultural value in church membership. Scarcity is not a commendable value when considering faith and money. These old ways of thinking have resulted in what has been called the annual lamentation of desperation. When mission and vision are not connected and the positive witness and encouragement of Scripture about the vital connection between faith and money is disregarded, the result is real despair in church leaders.

It seems a simple conclusion that if we continue thinking and acting about faith and money in the same old ways, we will undoubtedly get the same results. We think that if we just do what we have always done, but do it better and maybe be more committed to it, then we can somehow change the results. Over the years, many church leaders have said that the approach to faith and money for their church should be low key. This is usually a euphemism for a mediocre effort resulting from weariness and fear. It seems that we are paralyzed from thinking in new ways. So, how do we begin to change this dysfunctional paradigm?

A Better Way of Thinking

Eugene Grimm, in his excellent book *Generous People,* says that the three rules of stewardship ministries are to use a positive approach, to be faithful to the biblical message, and to focus on the mission, not the need. This would be a radical new way of thinking for many church leaders. A place to start changing the way we think is in Scripture. To overcome the common fear most church leaders have about connecting faith and money, we can find encouragement from 2 Timothy 1:7: "For God did not give us a spirit of cowardice, but rather a spirit of power and of love and of self-discipline." We can turn to the encouragement of Romans 12:2: "Be transformed by the renewing of your minds." In 2 Corinthians 8:5, Paul identifies the motivation for giving when reflecting on the extraordinarily generous response of the Macedonians: "They gave themselves first to the Lord."

And concerning our attitude, a verse that could help frame our thought process can be found in Philippians 4:8: "Finally, beloved, whatever is true, whatever is honorable, whatever is just, whatever is pure, whatever is pleasing, whatever is commendable, if there is any excellence and if there is anything worthy of praise, think about these things." These verses along with more than two thousand others that address faith and money, the source of truth, should be a starting place for changing the way we think.

Asking the Right Questions

More effective thought can begin by asking the right questions. It is amazing how little some church leaders know about their own church. Too often the wrong questions and analysis are used. When we compare how we did last year with how we are doing now, we often do not use an accurate method of analysis. Weekly and monthly comparisons are not useful because of holidays and five-Sunday months. Quarterly comparisons, on the other hand, can produce helpful information. Using the term *giving units* is common, but not really effective for analysis. The economic unit in our culture is the household, and one household might have several giving units. Another common dysfunctional approach is to take the church budget and divide it by weeks or months and define that as the weekly or monthly need. That is not accurate. Expenditures are not made by these time measurements, and giving is rarely done in equal weekly and monthly amounts. Fourth-quarter receipts often account for thirty to forty percent of the annual total. These approaches are common and complicate our understanding. Analysis using these approaches can prevent positive and bold planning.

The following questions can provide a starting point for analyzing a church's financial picture and getting in touch with the true stewardship status of the congregation:

1. What is the church's budget income in each quarter and year for the previous five years?
2. How many households are in the membership?
3. How many and what percentage of households pledge?
4. What percentage of last year's budget was pledged?
5. How many households gave more than one hundred dollars last year?
6. What percentage of households gave fifty percent of the budget receipts last year?
7. What percentage of households gave eighty percent of the budget receipts last year?
8. What percentage of budget receipts came from households with adults aged fifty-five or over? aged seventy-five or over?
9. What is the approximate percentage of income given to the church? (Use available demographic research to determine the average household income of church members. Multiply that average by the number of households in the church. Then divide the budget income from last year by that number.)
10. How is the budget communicated to the membership?
11. How are the ongoing church finances reported to the members throughout the year?
12. What kind of annual campaign does the church conduct?
13. When is the church campaign conducted? Why is that time selected?
14. Who is responsible for the church campaign?
15. What does the church do for stewardship education?
16. Is there stewardship education for all ages?
17. What is the church's greatest stewardship need?
18. What is currently planned and calendared to address that need?

19. Does the church have a leadership group, other than the finance committee, to lead stewardship?
20. Does the church have stewardship sermons and statements of support throughout the year?

These analysis questions can help leaders identify relevant facts about their church. Each church has its own history and culture about money. With understanding, steps can be taken to affirm the positive accomplishments and address areas of need.

Equipping Clergy

Although each church is different, resources often focus on a common approach to stewardship for all churches. Usually, these efforts are focused on the average size church, make assumptions of common experience and values, and make recommendations that often do not fit the church. These designs also often make assumptions that the church leaders and members are aware of and supportive of denominational programs and priorities. That assumption is a significant leap of faith in many churches. Deviating from the standardized approach requires some thinking that often has not been cultivated. Some success has been found when denominations identify starting points and resources based on a church's size. Another approach that has yielded some positive results is an attempt to equip the clergy to better understand a relevant theology of stewardship. A starting point for equipping clergy can be the use of some basic discussion questions as well as the identification of some resources for further growth. The following questions have been used with small groups of clergy:

1. What forces have shaped your attitude about the connection of faith and money?
2. What is your personal theological perspective about faith and money?
3. What is the basis of this theological perspective?
4. What is your personal experience with faith and money?
5. What is the largest cash gift you have ever made?
6. Have you ever made a gift or financial commitment to the church that caused you to give up something you valued?
7. As a pastor, what is your vocational experience in faith and money?
8. In your opinion, what is the major biblical teaching about giving?
9. What is the best sermon you have ever heard about faith and money?
10. What is the greatest obstacle to understanding faith and money in your church?

11. With regard to faith and money, which of the following best describes your own thoughts?
    - intentional or incidental
    - proactive or reactive
    - a process of growth in discipleship or a seasonal event

An honest evaluation of how we think as individuals will equip us to advance beyond our present, often fearful, attitude. It can help us move beyond a theology and attitude based on scarcity and toward a biblical theology based on the abundance of God's blessings and gifts. Then we can become equipped as clergy, and as lay leaders too, to lead with boldness and conviction.

For Further Study

"Checklist for Vital Stewardship," "Analyzing Your Congregation's Potential," and "Preparing a Tally of Appeal Results," Appendices A, B, and D in *Generous People: How To Encourage Vital Stewardship,* by Eugene Grimm (Abingdon Press, 1992).

"Creating a Climate for Giving," Chapter 1 in *Creating a Climate for Giving,* by Donald W. Joiner (Discipleship Resources, 2001).

"Doctor's Orders: Ten Things to Do When You Think You Have Done It All," Chapter 9 in *Get Well! Stay Well! Prescriptions for a Financially Healthy Congregation,* by Wayne C. Barrett (Discipleship Resources, 1997).

How to Increase Giving in Your Church: A Practical Guide to the Sensitive Task of Raising Money for Your Church or Ministry, by George Barna (Regal Books, 1997).

Revolutionizing Christian Stewardship for the 21st Century: Lessons From Copernicus, by Dan R. Dick (Discipleship Resources, 1997).

Chapter Ten

Relevant Questions

S ome of our best thinking is often provoked when we ask relevant
questions. As we begin to consider how to proceed in stewardship
planning for a local church, we have to begin to focus. Identifying the
basic components of an annual campaign and asking relevant questions about
each component can provide critical direction. Even the choice of a particular
campaign resource can be more meaningful if we start the planning process
with some good thinking about the answers to relevant questions.

What Is the Purpose of the Campaign?

The first general question is, What is the purpose or desired outcome of
our efforts? Why have an annual campaign at all? While we will consider
the year-round approach, the focus time of a campaign is still valuable in
most churches. The quick response to the question is, Because we want
people to make commitments so that the finance committee can plan the
church's budget. But that answer will most often lead to a campaign that
requires nominal effort and will probably yield results that look a lot like
last year's outcomes.

A stronger perspective is that the purpose of the annual faith and money
campaign is to create, reinforce, and promote vision and vitality in the
congregation. In essence, it is a guided faith journey that can complement all

the other year-round approaches to stewardship education and ministry awareness. If that is the fundamental purpose, then the campaign will require effort and organization, and the outcome will be significantly different from the usual response. The difference will be because more prayerful planning, thoughtful organization, creative imagination, and careful implementation have gone into the effort. Even if last year's campaign was a blockbuster, this campaign will be different because the vision for ministry *next* year will be different from the vision for ministry *this* year. If a reasonable case cannot be made for that proposition, then maybe the various ministry planning leaders in the congregation need to go back to the spiritual drawing board before a campaign is ever planned and conducted. If our vision for the new year is maintaining status quo, where is the sense of continuing revelation? We ought to be able to identify which ministries are being expanded, which ones are being curtailed, and what new ministries are required. When the ministry leaders have prayerfully and openly sought God's direction and developed plans accordingly, then it is time to plan a campaign to explain and interpret that vision. The difference between these two approaches is passion. Is the annual campaign just a recurring event to raise funds, or is it a vital part of an ongoing process of discipleship, individually and corporately? A recurring idea in the writing of Paul is relevant here, as he encourages people to have one mind, to be of one accord, and to have a common purpose (Philippians 2:2).

How Can We Design a Creative Campaign?

A creative and vibrant campaign can be designed in a congregation by a relatively small team of imaginative and diligent members, who move through a series of questions and shape the campaign as they devise answers. Consider these eight planning components as a guide in developing an appropriate and faithful approach. Respond to the questions in each category to sharpen the focus. It is important to use all of the components, since omission of any of them will diminish the best and most successful outcome.

1. Creating Vision
a. What is the scope of ministry for our congregation next year?
b. What new ministries are being proposed, and why are they important?
c. What excites us?
d. What will excite other members and friends about the ministries of our church?
e. What are the distinctive characteristics of our church?
f. How will we emphasize these things during the campaign and throughout the coming year?

2. Gathering Information

a. What does the congregation need to understand in order to make informed decisions about their support of the ministries (not the budget) of our church?

b. How will the necessary information be gathered, and how can it be conveyed to both the heads and hearts of members and friends of our congregation?

c. Who will collect stories about how the ministries of our congregation have made a difference in people's lives this year?

3. Establishing a Biblical, Theological, and Spiritual Foundation

a. How will Scripture inform us as we grow as stewards of the resources God has provided for us?

b. What is the particular biblical passage, story, or verse on which the campaign will be built? How will it give the endeavor faithful relevance and focus the thrust and vitality of the campaign?

c. Is there biblical truth that can become a viable theme of the campaign or a framework for it?

d. How can and will the planning group be the prayerful, spiritual nucleus of the campaign?

4. Planning Our Intensive Phase

a. How will the information about the projected ministries of the congregation be communicated in ways that emerge from our theological foundation and engage people on a personal level?

b. Exactly what materials will we need to develop to tell the congregation's story and to cast the vision of ministry for our new year?

c. What time period will be our primary intensive phase of the emphasis?

d. How will members and friends be invited to respond and make their commitments?

e. What reluctance can we expect from members of the congregation, and how will we address those issues?

f. What questions do we anticipate, and how will we answer them?

5. Mobilizing Our Resources

a. Who will need to do what and when, in order to implement the process we have designed?

b. What is our specific, reliable, week-by-week timeline for the preparation of all materials, deadlines for printing, and mailing dates for letters and distribution of materials?

c. How much will it cost, and how will it be paid for?

d. What system of accountability will we have to assure that tasks are completed on schedule and that costs are within our guidelines?

6. Conveying Inspiration

a. What will inspire members and friends to engage in the campaign, to devotedly reflect and discern how God would have them respond in commitment?

b. How will we guide the congregation to pray about their individual and family commitments?

c. What resources do we need to develop to support the spiritual growth of members and friends?

7. Anticipating Celebration

a. When is Commitment Day? How will we receive commitments from the congregation?

b. How will we inform and excite the congregation about our Commitment Day?

c. How will we follow up with those who have not yet made their commitments? When will we begin and end this follow-up? Who will do it? How, when, and by whom will they be trained?

d. How will we bring joyful, celebrative completion to the endeavors that will be appropriate to the culture of our congregation, authentic to our scriptural heritage, and inspiring to our congregation as a whole?

8. Remaining Thankful

a. How will we acknowledge every commitment made to the projected ministries of our church?

b. Is our financial record keeping effective and efficient, or do we need to make changes before we begin our new fiscal year?

c. How will we maintain the flow of current, accurate, motivational, and legally compliant information about individual, familial, and congregational support throughout the year?

When the process of planning the annual campaign assumes a format of asking and responding to questions, the potential for creativity rises dramatically. The questions in these eight planning components will beget others. However, in place of plotting out a dreary campaign that is simply facts and a lot of figures, these flowing questions have many points at which the imaginative, energizing, and engaging talents of congregational members will burst forth.

What Comes After the Campaign?

Note that, at several points in the succession of questions, reference is made to actions to be taken during the year. Often, when a campaign is completed and the commitment cards are in, the campaign is considered complete. The finance committee takes over and moves on. Keeping the campaign connected with the ministries that happen in the months that follow the campaign establishes a credibility on which the next campaign may be built. One difficulty that congregations encounter in planning a campaign is that no positive connection is made between commitments that are made during a campaign and the reporting of subsequent fulfillment of those commitments. In other words, how monies are used to impact and change lives. Even though it may not be the responsibility of the team planning the faith and money campaign to provide that connection, the team can assert itself to be sure that the mechanisms are in place for those tasks to be performed before it comes time for the next campaign.

Chapter Eleven

Ideas for the Annual Campaign

T he progression of the relevant questions and the resulting answers can provide a sound direction and, along the way, provoke some creative ideas for your church. This chapter could be called "The Best Ideas Ever"; but since any idea must fit into a culture of stewardship within a church, a broader discussion of some key concepts might be more helpful. One of the problems with offering great ideas is the tendency so many have to clone an idea without understanding it conceptually, which can lead to taking shortcuts that diminish the potential value of the idea. It is not unusual to see the success of an idea at one church and be disappointed when that idea cannot be transplanted to another church. It is important to identify what might best fit a particular church.

Personal Experiences

One great idea is the use of testimonies or statements of support from personal experiences with giving. However, this practice often translates into a senior adult couple waxing eloquent about tithing for the last fifty years, and the message does not get through. Or we have a well-intentioned person who gives a speech that is abstract or laden with symbols or church talk that fills a lot of time and goes on and on. It seems almost irreverent to suggest a guideline and rehearsal for statements of support, but some focus would help.

A simple, written guideline for anyone who speaks and an opportunity to rehearse would enhance the traditional statement of support.

The experiences of members could be used in other ways that would be helpful. One alternative to the traditional speech approach is to have a panel of three or four people representing the various demographics or ages of your membership. An articulate moderator could interview them or lead a panel discussion to answer some basic questions, such as these:

- How did you learn about giving?
- What is the greatest challenge in your giving?
- What is the greatest joy in giving?
- What motivates you to increase your giving?

Ministry Awareness Opportunities

Another modification of the panel idea is to have a panel that informs the congregation about various ministries within the church. This ministry communication can help put a face with a program. Individuals can give ministry testimonies, and those who are hesitant to speak can express themselves through the written word. These written testimonies, using the same format of questions, can be used as bulletin or newsletter inserts.

Creating and achieving ministry awareness has already been presented as a challenge. The use of a narrative budget and of ministry testimonies can be helpful in making the connection between faith and money. Another way to build awareness is by having a fall festival or a ministry fair, which is a tradition in many churches. The ministry fair is not a new concept, but, if done well, it can have a tremendous impact in both motivation and education. Set aside a specific time in the year for the church to bring a special focus to ministries served. One church, in lieu of worship, designates an entire day for the fair and celebration. They use the fellowship hall and a big-top tent. Trade-show-like displays hosted by ministry participants allow people to walk through and get information first person about the various ways the church ministers in the community and beyond. Handouts that help make the connection between faith and money include the costs of providing particular ministries. After walking through the ministry fair, one longtime church member said that he had no idea before the fair about the breadth and depth of ministries that the church provided. While the ministry fair might not fit a particular church culture, the usual hesitation is usually about something other than a violation of something held sacred. In the Old Testament, a special annual tithe was committed to celebration for a reason. Our spiritual journey, individually and corporately, is to be worthy of celebration.

A Fireside Chat

When a church has had difficulty addressing the issue of faith and money and has no positive tradition to build on, a fireside chat has worked. This idea calls for the senior pastor to change the dynamic of worship. When it is time for the sermon, the pastor sits down in an easy chair on the platform with a microphone and simply tells about his or her own pilgrimage with faith and money. This sort of candid, less-formal approach can catch people off guard and create a strong teachable moment. Simply by recognizing that the subject of faith and money has been difficult for the church, perhaps the pastor can open the door to a discussion of the spiritual issues surrounding stewardship. This approach is an excellent way to counter the church culture that prides itself on never talking about money. Taking this approach outside of a campaign season, perhaps during Lent, can help make the spiritual connection even stronger.

Four-Week, Four-Card

Another way to get into a positive expression and celebration about faith and money is to use what some churches have done in a four-week, four-card approach. The first week church members receive a letter with a challenge to think about what they love most about the church and to write it down on an enclosed index card. The next Sunday the cards are brought to a designated bulletin board and put up for a display. The second week another letter is sent requesting that the members write on the enclosed card the name of a person in the church who has meant a lot to them. The next Sunday the cards are added to those from the previous week. The third week the letter requests that members think about what one new thing they would like to see happen in the church for the coming year. When those cards are added the following Sunday, the bulletin board becomes a real focus of celebration. Worship services can be focused on related themes. The final week a letter can be sent that says: "With regard to what you love, who you love, and what you want to see happen, what do you believe God wants to give through you this year?" The pledge card will be received in the worship service the following Sunday. This idea helps a church that might have some history of aversion to the use of a commitment card, and it can change the dynamic of supporting a church budget to a consideration of participating in a celebration. Churches that have used this approach have supplemented the letters with stewardship cartoon kiosks, bulletin inserts, verbal responses to the cards each week in worship, newsletter summaries the week after a response, and even faith and money games, such as acrostics and crossword puzzles.

Focus on Age Levels

Some ideas should focus on age-group interests. For instance, get senior adults in touch with what is happening in the areas of ministry that pertain to children and youth. Taking senior adults on tours of children and youth areas during Sunday school or having children and youth make presentations to senior adults during fellowships or Sunday school might be helpful. While there is value to a youth group or mission group telling the church in worship about their work, a more targeted effort can allow questions and clarifications. Some churches have used various kinds of adoption programs, where senior-adult classes adopt a specific children's group or youth group with which to be involved and to mentor.

Another idea is to have the children participate in a special part of a campaign. One early-elementary children's Sunday school class was challenged to make a poster or banner to use in a parade in worship. It involved instruction in the Sunday school about faith and money and some activity at home as well. On the concluding Sunday, the children marched in from the back of the sanctuary during a congregational hymn. As they came down the aisles of the church, they turned and faced the congregation, proudly displaying their work. Banners and posters of every size and quality had messages, such as: "Got Stewardship?" "Give Money!" "For God So Loved the World He Gave." The congregation enjoyed it, the parents had been involved, and the message was charming as well as challenging.

It is important that the church understand that each age group within the congregation offers many teachable moments for learning about what God has to say about stewardship and commitment. For example, when youth are moving through their teenage years, making the connection between faith and money is not something that comes naturally, especially in our consumer culture. Indeed, it is shocking to learn how much disposable income is in the hands of our youth. The merchants know it, and one need only to visit an area mall on the weekend to see it firsthand.

Teaching youth and children the importance of making and keeping commitments will position them for more productive lives and mentor them in responsible stewardship. People from all age groups have personal faith stories that can stir our hearts and inspire renewed commitment. Whether a child, youth, single adult, young family, middle-aged family, or senior adult, everyone can grow in his or her personal understanding of Christian discipleship. Becoming responsible stewards of time, talent, and treasure is a crucial part of the life cycle of maturing discipleship. When the church focuses on various life circumstances represented by the demographics of the congregation and targets and creates stewardship educational opportunities, significant advances result. Consider some of the following ideas:

1. Take an intentional approach in planning educational emphases for all ages.
2. Use a narrative budget to communicate ministry opportunities that connect faith and money.
3. Use tried and proven-successful resources, such as the Bible, to teach stewardship and to target resources for life situations. For example, many scriptural references include children. Such stories capture the imaginations of the children to think about ways of helping others and honoring Christ. Include stewardship examples during children's time.
4. Suggest that families allow the children and youth to participate in the offering by placing the families' gift in the offering plate.
5. Create a team to look at everything done in worship as it relates to stewardship through the eyes of laity, including the children. Identify any seemingly confusing rituals that can be improved by participation, and maximize times that can enrich the experience.
6. Provide for church members envelopes of information, including suggestions for parents about how they can encourage the faith experience for children and teach systematic giving.
7. Model and teach tithing in the church and at home.
8. Include children and youth in the annual faith and money campaign by creating special commitment cards that target their life situation.
9. Teach various ways for senior adults to give financially to support the work of the church through various gifts in kind and planned gifts that in the long run can improve their own life situations while advancing God's work.
10. Provide special-focus seminars on financial management for senior adults, families of all ages, children, and youth.
11. Advocate personal responsible money management that recognizes that God owns it all and that teaches what the Bible has to say about responsible stewardship.
12. Encourage parents to consider including youth in the management of family finances, in order to mentor understanding of money management.
13. Include people of all ages in congregational budget planning and oversight.
14. Provide effective tools and training that equip church leaders and parents to convey the stewardship message.
15. Support and encourage young adults and youth in developing a responsible work ethic.
16. Teach ancillary financial skills.

17. Make it easy for people to give by using automatic bank withdrawals. This practice is also helpful to church planning because it helps to even out giving, over the summer months in particular.
18. Create greater awareness of giving by sending monthly statements. Include spiritually motivating materials to encourage and affirm faithful stewardship. When a young family that is living from paycheck to paycheck gets behind on a financial commitment, it is difficult for the family to make it up. Sometimes being behind becomes a negative, hopeless factor that results in the family simply giving up.
19. Offer credit card options for members who indicate that this would be helpful to them.
20. Plan regular stewardship sermons at different times throughout the year, not just during the annual stewardship emphasis.
21. Use existing educational venues to teach biblically-based stewardship throughout the year.

Many good ideas and effective programs are available to use in teaching stewardship. But to make the connection between faith and money in a specific congregation, ideas have to be adapted. This is one of the reasons that it is important to have the right leadership. In the end, consistent education, paired with spiritual inspiration, moves the church to a deeper understanding of stewardship and higher levels of giving and discipleship.

For Further Study

105 Questions Children Ask About Money Matters, by Daryl J. Lucas (Tyndale House, 1997).

"The Annual 'Stewardship' Appeal—Method vs. Values," Chapter XIII in *The Passionate Steward: Recovering Christian Stewardship From Secular Fundraising,* by Michael O'Hurley-Pitts (St. Brigid Press, 2001).

Dollars and Sense for Kids, by Janet Bodnar (Kiplinger Books, 1999).

Growing Up Generous: Engaging Youth in Giving and Serving, by Eugene C. Roehlkepartain, Elanah Delyah Naftali, and Laura Musegades (Alban Institute, 2000).

Kids and Money: Giving Them the Savvy to Succeed Financially, by Jayne A. Pearl (Bloomberg Press, 1999).

A Penny Saved: Teaching Your Children the Values and Life Skills They Will Need to Live in the Real World, by Neale S. Godfrey (Simon and Schuster, 1995).

Chapter Twelve

The Value of a Year-Round Plan

I f we are really going to raise the level of our theological discourse and experience with faith and money, then we need to rethink the traditional model of money being a needs-based seasonal event. Dr. Karl Menninger, in his book *Whatever Happened to Sin?,* captured the spirit of the struggle of teaching faithful stewardship when he asked how we can help people shift from greed to generosity. He went on to say that greed can be an incurable disease. The church is given the mandate to make disciples and is responsible for teaching the whole truth about faith and money so that it becomes embedded in the life of the faithful disciple.

A New Paradigm: A Year-Round Emphasis

To translate faith and money into a consideration of discipleship, a more sweeping and intentional consideration must be made. This will not be easy in a church culture that often suggests that any talk about money is too much. We must develop a radically new paradigm where faith and money is not a primary consideration of funding a budget but of living out our Christian lives. Ideas such as separating the budget communication and the time of financial response can create a lot of anxiety. If we had a leadership group dedicated to the one task of stewardship, how might we plan out a full year of addressing faith and money?

Sometimes church leaders say they would prefer a year-round stewardship approach, thinking it would enable them to escape the stewardship demands placed on them during the traditional financial campaign period. However, in the year-round approach, church leaders have the great responsibility of making sure details are implemented. Failure to consistently work the plan yields low response. Each month in the year-round approach has specific tasks, including congregational communication, sermons, educational venues, seminars, workshops, and the creation and use of other inspirational tools.

One church leader had some success implementing a modified year-round program using the anniversary date of members to follow up on their pledge renewal. When the same pastor attempted to implement this approach in another congregation, it fell flat. The culture and demographics of the church are critical factors in choosing the best stewardship program approach.

Where Do We Start?

The year-round approach should begin with some critical analysis using the tools suggested in Chapter Ten. Understanding the historical and existing facts is a starting point. Unfortunately, a lot of planning is begun with assumptions and old wives' tales, more so than with real empirical data. The leadership group charged with the responsibility for implementing the year-round plan should begin by identifying every financial activity, including every letter, mailing, announcement, lesson, sermon, special offering, age-group-based or ministry-based fundraiser, budget development, financial report, and offertory throughout the previous year. Identifying all of these activities is a challenging task for most leadership groups. The church's tendency to deal with financial matters in a series of unconnected events makes it difficult to remember all that has been done. It is this unconnectedness that is precisely the point. Let's identify the real sacred cows, the things we must do. Then we can choose to do things that can make the most difference.

Consideration should begin with a discussion and evaluation of what needs to be done to emphasize stewardship weekly, monthly, quarterly, semiannually, annually, and in special seasons. If a church has a traditional Easter or Christmas offering, does it still serve a purpose? If the church has some denominationally mandated offerings, can they serve as educational opportunities? Is the offertory a rote, meaningless time in the worship or a time of deep inspiration that connects faith and money? Taking an objective look at these issues is not easy, as the first response is to defend everything we have always done as though change is heresy.

Recently, a task force was asked to review the eighteen special offerings that had evolved from the state and national denominational leaders. Each of the offerings had decreased in revenue over the last few years, but none had been eliminated. The leaders defended various offerings, even though some no longer served their purpose. The result was an inability to recommend any meaningful changes.

When considering a twelve-month plan for a local church, list all the variables, including subjects and settings of value to the congregation. These variables can be identified through the relevant questions in Chapter Ten. If the multi-task financial leadership group has been developed, consideration can be given to annual, capital, and planned giving; various approaches to age-group stewardship education; special offerings; fundraising events; systems of communication and reporting; and budget development and management. If this approach is used, the pastor needs to be encouraged and given more freedom to preach more often and more boldly about the related subjects that connect faith and money.

One Model for a Year-Round Plan

The problem with offering a model of what a year-round plan might include is that someone will try to start with the model to develop a plan. The model suggested on pages 82–85 might have some elements that are relevant for your church and yet entirely overlook other critical subjects vital to your church. Note the resources for further study, listed below, to see other models and approaches.

If the church is serious about using a year-round stewardship plan, a specific staff person should be assigned to oversee and monitor the implementation of the plan and to serve as the catalyst for action. If this is not possible, the plan's implementation may be impaired. Even though the church may be using a year-round approach to stewardship, the congregation must ultimately be asked to formalize their intent to be faithful stewards. Therefore, a commitment time is recommended.

For Further Study

"Developing an Annual Stewardship Plan," Chapter 4 in *Developing a Giving Church,* by Stan Toler and Elmer L. Towns (Beacon Hill Press, 1999).

"Implementing a 12-Month Stewardship Plan," Chapter 8 in *Creating Congregations of Generous People,* by Michael Durall (Alban Institute, 1999).

"Stewards in Action: The Journey Is Our Home," Chapter 4 in *Afire With God: Spirit-ed Stewardship for a New Century,* by Betsy Schwarzentraub (Discipleship Resources, 2000).

Model of an Annual Year of Stewardship

January

- Mail a faith-and-finance report with the annual contribution record for the previous year. This piece gives a simple financial report showing the total pledged and unpledged income for the year, expenses for the year, and balances for the end of the year.

- Mail (and possibly preach) a state-of-the-church letter from the pastor to members of the congregation. This letter thanks people for their contributions for the last year and summarizes the ministry accomplishments that have been possible because of their faithfulness in giving. Then express gratitude for this year's pledges. If pledges have not been received, thank the people in advance for their continued and growing faithfulness in financial support. Highlight ministry opportunities for the coming year. Enclose a contribution envelope in the mailing.

> *The faith-and-finance report and the state-of-the-church letter mailings can be combined; but each needs to be one page, with 12-point or larger type. These mailings should not be included in other church publications, such as the newsletter or the Sunday bulletin.*

- The pastor and a member of the permanent fund committee visit a planned-giving prospect. (Planned giving includes a bequest, a trust, an annuity, or an outright gift.)

February

- Host a weekend (or week) of personal finance workshops, which can include a workshop for personal financial management, a wills and bequests workshop, a children's financial project, and a youth workshop. Another approach would be for the congregation to watch and discuss the video *Wesley and Giving* (United Methodist Communications, 888-346-3862, item #843433).

- The pastor and a member of the permanent fund committee visit a planned-giving prospect.

March

- Preach a stewardship message as a part of the Lenten season. This message may address personal priorities or the meaning of prayers, presence, gifts, and service.

- The permanent fund committee follows up with a mailing to those who attended the February wills and bequests workshop. This contact is a simple thank-you for attending and a clarification about how and when they can receive additional information.

- The pastor and a member of the permanent fund committee visit a planned-giving prospect.

April

- Mail a faith-and-finance report with the first-quarter contribution statement. Review the receipts, expenses, and ministry accomplishments of the first quarter. The more human faces that can be related to the finances, the better the report. Finally, preview the late-spring and summer ministries. Enclose a contribution envelope in the mailing.
- The pastor and a member of the permanent fund committee visit a planned-giving prospect.

May

- Mail a letter between Mother's Day and Memorial Day to preview the activities planned for the summer months. Then challenge people to leave their contributions before they take their vacation. (The reality is that people take their contributions with them and do not bring them back, which is one reason many churches have a summer slump in contributions.) Enclose a contribution envelope in the mailing.
- The stewardship committee meets to begin planning the fall campaign. If the finance committee has this responsibility, a subcommittee should be appointed. The subcommittee may include some non-committee members for this task. People who need to help in stewardship are teachers, sales people, public relations professionals, and other creative people.
- The pastor and a member of the permanent fund committee visit a planned-giving prospect.

June

- Emphasize the Make-Your-Will Month with direct mailings and visuals.
- The pastor and a member of the permanent fund committee visit a planned-giving prospect.

July

- Mail the second-quarter contribution record with a faith-and-finance report, which briefly highlights the income and expenses and compares them with the second quarter last year. In this report tell one story about a recipient of a ministry of the church and the difference the ministry made in his or her life.
- The pastor and a member of the permanent fund committee visit a planned-giving prospect.

August

- The finance committee or budget development committee distributes budget request forms for the next year to all ministry leaders. After reviewing income projections for the year, the finance committee decides whether a September or December special offering is needed. This review will allow appropriate planning for a better solicitation.
- The pastor and a member of the permanent fund committee visit a planned-giving prospect.

September

- The finance committee considers whether a back-to-school mailing is needed to review summer accomplishments, preview fall activities, and solicit a catch-up offering. Do not suggest a catch-up offering casually. If it is needed because of significant summer shortfall, then it ought to be well communicated and promoted. Unless there is a dire need, an end-of-year offering will yield greater results.
- The finance committee receives budget requests from ministry leaders and begins to put together a preliminary budget.
- The stewardship committee continues their planning for October through November while beginning ministry testimonies after Labor Day.
- Mail targeted planned-giving information to a specific planned-giving prospects database.
- The pastor and a member of the permanent fund committee visit a planned-giving prospect.

October

- A faith-and-finance report is sent with a third-quarter contribution record. This report previews the fourth-quarter activities, including the stewardship campaign currently underway.
- The finance committee and administrative board approve the line-item budget, and the stewardship committee translates the line-item budget into a narrative budget.
- The leadership group should be challenged upon budget approval to make their pledges first. This challenge may be made in the administrative board meeting or in a fellowship setting with more focus, intentionality, and challenge. If there needs to be a growth in giving, it must be modeled by leaders.
- The stewardship committee continues to have ministry testimonies in worship services and small groups. The committee begins using visual

resources, such as posters, bulletin boards, information booths, videos, and bulletin inserts.
- The pastor and a member of the permanent fund committee visit a planned-giving prospect.

November

- The stewardship committee mails a narrative budget to every family in the church. Ministry testimonies continue. In place of stewardship testimonies, a panel of givers representing all ages will be interviewed in a worship service using such questions as: Why do you give to the church? How do you decide how much to give? How did you learn about giving? What is the greatest challenge in giving? What is the greatest joy in giving? Written stewardship testimonies may also be used as bulletin inserts or as newsletter inserts.
- The pastor preaches at least one, preferably two, messages on giving.
- Commitment Day is the day to receive pledges for the coming year. This day should focus only on the financial pledge, not on prayers, presence, and service.
- The pastor and a member of the permanent fund committee visit a planned-giving prospect.

December

- After the last day of contribution in November, a mailing is prepared as a conclusion for the year. A faith-and-finance report is developed with a report of the annual campaign results. A record of contribution for the first eleven months is sent with a challenge to end the year appropriately. Include an offering envelope. If the church has an annual Christmas offering, promote that offering with this mailing.
- The pastor writes personal letters to the planned-giving prospects visited during the year, wishing them a Merry Christmas and a Happy New Year and encouraging them to reflect on the visit and the planned gift discussed.

Chapter Thirteen

Sources and Resources

A nother way to provoke creative thinking about faith and money is to begin to identify the sources and resources available. *Sources* are places where thinking and resource development happen. *Resources* are the products available from all of the sources.

Begin With Caution

Since thinking is such a challenge in this area, one warning seems necessary: Narrowing the search for sources and resources to one writer or venue or exclusively to one's own denominational materials will severely limit thinking and restrict creativity. Every church is unique, and effective communication must be sensitive to the church's unique personality. So, broaden your search and evaluate a variety of sources and resources before making a choice. The point is to be willing to think in new ways.

Correspondingly, just because someone found a publisher to print his or her work does not mean that every word printed on the topic of faith and money is worthwhile. Some really poor scholarship in this area focuses on method and delivery instead of on cogent biblical, theological, and pragmatic application. The key is to develop a basic theology of stewardship through which you can discern those resources of value.

What About Consulting Groups?

Professional consulting groups can be one helpful source. Some of the best practical results have been found in relationship with professionals. However, make sure that you always do the necessary homework on the group's track record. The men and women who serve in these consulting companies bring a lot of experience to the table. It is difficult to get beyond the sales attitude often demonstrated in the presentation of their services, so hiring the right consultant requires asking a lot of questions of the individual who will be the on-site working consultant. The company, whether a small one- or two-person entity or a regional company or national firm, is only as strong as the person from the company who works with you. What is his or her background, training, giftedness, track record, and spiritual maturity? Be clear about your expectations and theirs before hiring someone.

Don't Overlook Local Stewards

A source that is often overlooked is that person or family in your community of faith who has had a great personal experience in the area of faith and money. The person who has the gift of giving and gifts of communication, organization, leadership, and teaching can often provide helpful and relevant leadership to a local church's effort. That person may also be the type of person who can discern what resources best fit the congregation. Statements of support from that person can challenge hearts and raise horizons. The faithful experience of other Christians can motivate and benefit the whole body of Christ.

Read Numerous Written Materials

Books, articles, and other written materials can be found through a lot of different publishers. Some denominational publications can provide excellent insights and offer research and scholarly considerations about faith and money. These are not always written or researched by theologians. Sometimes sociologists can provide some critically important observations, and leaders from other walks of life can identify some helpful insights. In the last decade, some substantial research has been funded and documented that allows a better understanding of the root challenges and systemic disconnections that complicate the task of addressing faith and money issues. Understanding the facts from an articulate economist can be helpful as well. The categories for these resources may include theology of stewardship, annual stewardship, stewardship studies, vision with both forecasting and renewal, budget development, marketing, communication, personal money management, affluence and major gifts, capital campaigns, preaching and teaching resources, church administration, leadership and management, and retirement. Some of the individual books have been identified at the end of some of the chapters in this book, and other sources have been listed at the end of this chapter.

Watch Videos

Closely associated with books, articles, and other written materials are video productions. Helpful videos addressing research, financial management, faith and money issues particular to a denomination's heritage and values, missional presentations, and biblical instruction can all provide additional resources for leaders. Many churches have found a great value in producing their own videos and presenting both instruction and a case statement for financial support.

Search the Internet

The Internet is an excellent source available to everyone. Through the resource lists of publishers, denominations, agencies, associations and institutes, websites can be identified and links to other websites can be listed. Books, studies, training opportunities, curriculum recommendations, research, creative ideas, discussions, and preaching resources can all be found through exploring the Internet.

How Do We Sort Through It All?

Not too long ago, a list of sources and resources for faith and money was presented to a group of state leaders from one denomination. One of the leaders felt overwhelmed with the identification of so many available resources and asked how a starting point could be identified. The frustrated request was couched with the words: "I do not have time to read all this stuff, so is there one resource you would recommend." Unfortunately, this question is an all-too-common response. Many leaders prefer to try to identify a magic bullet to address faith and money and really do not want to think beyond that level. It would be helpful if a small group of leaders came together and each read a book or resource and reported on its message at a subsequent meeting. Some assignments could be made to prepare for a planned brainstorming session. If our position is to be limited by a single resource or by a minimum of time, we will continue to relegate the consideration of faith and money issues to an insignificant place in Christian life. The encouragement is that if a leader really wants to learn and grow in this area, more than enough sources and resources are available.

Look at Helpful Websites

Some other sources that should be reviewed are agencies, associations, and institutes that have focused on faith and money issues on a broader scale than one denomination. These are often multi-denominational sources that consider various issues that churches face across the country. Their research, observations, workshops, and resources are often helpful and adaptable. Here is a beginning list of such groups.

Abingdon Press (*www.abingdonpress.com*)

Alban Institute (*www.alban.org*)

Christian Stewardship Association (*www.stewardship.org*)

Cokesbury (*www.cokesbury.com*)

Crown Financial Ministries (*www.crown.org*)

Discipleship Resources (*www.discipleshipresources.org*)

EcuFilm (*www.ecufilm.org*)

Ecumenical Stewardship Center (*www.stewardshipresources.org*)

Jossey-Bass (*www.josseybass.com*)

LeWay Resources (*www.leway.net/Index.htm*)

National Association of Church Business Administration (*www.nacba.net*)

Resource Services, Inc. (*www.rsi-ketchum.com/index2.asp*)

Chapter Fourteen

Stewardship Stories of Angst, Anger, and Apathy

W hether at the level of an individual or a congregation, attitudes toward stewardship are often marked by angst, anger, and apathy.

One Church's Story

A small church needed to build a family life center to serve the needs of its youth. Other than the community school, the church youth program provided the only possible means for recreation, wholesome fellowship, and fun. The building plan was born in the hearts of some of the members who saw and embraced the vision of what the church could become, given adequate facilities for ministry. Additionally, the church roof leaked like a sieve, leaving the sanctuary ceiling spotted with unsightly yellow rings. During the rains, the pinging sound of rain dripping in pots placed around the floor and on the pews nearly drowned out the ringing of the bells.

By all appearances and evaluative measures, this conservative congregation had all the resources needed to build the proposed facility, plus replace the roof. However, members had become polarized either for or against the new project. The primary interest among those opposed to the project was infighting over what should or should not be done. The project had become a tool for power and control.

Initial signals revealed startling evidence of critical spirits and unkind attitudes toward one another, their pastor, and anyone who dared to offer assistance to them. One member remarked, "I hope you don't come in here and start talking about God's will, because this project has nothing to do with God. It is the pastor's idea, along with a few misdirected do-gooders." The speaker accused the pastor of trying to make the church into a city church, of which he wanted no part. "This is our church, and the pastor will not always be here. We can outlast him."

Certain members in the church effectively fueled the flame of passionate disunity by effectively using the local telephone party line as a weapon of mass destruction. Those who favored the building plan watched in amazement and dismay as the venom poured freely from their lifelong friends and neighbors. In the end, no one wanted to see the church split. Those who favored the project were wiling to give up their vision for greater ministry in order to keep peace in the family. Who knows how long some congregations will need to wander around in the wilderness until the naysayers die off and the faithful can proceed to the Promised Land.

What about the roof? We predicted that, after hearing our professional opinion that the church should not proceed with a campaign to fund the building project, some in the church would move with haste to gather up the $23,000 needed for the new roof. To further ensure this would happen, we gave back to the church the last portion of our professional fee for work done up to that point so that it could be applied toward the roof. Looking back, I do not recall any specific comments of gratitude from the crowd, though I did get quite a number of letters from members apologizing for the conduct of other members in the church. Later, the pastor told me that our gift was the largest one made toward getting the roof project completed. The Lord continues to work in mysterious ways.

Overcoming the Roadblocks

Step back for a moment and consider this: When a church is doing something extraordinary for the cause of Christ, spiritual warfare can be expected. Unless the congregation recognizes the possibility of spiritual warfare as a scriptural phenomenon and takes steps at the outset to prepare spiritually to oppose it, it will be devastating. God equips people to accomplish the visions for ministry inspired by the Spirit, but the journey is not free of roadblocks.

Too often, people place God's work in the last position on the list of personal priorities, not even close to their own desires. One woman unashamedly exclaimed that the church should understand that members have their own plans and need: "While I am all for the church having the money it needs to operate, we are not able to give anything more because we are planning to go to Europe. We are going to build a new house, and we don't even know what that will cost yet. I know that the church is growing and has many needs. And while I hope it all goes well, I can't give right now until I know what is left over. I will pray for the church, if that helps." Do you suppose it is easier to give when one's resources are less and consequently the gift amount is less?

Before receiving the news of Christ, we are all without true hope and joy. Once we receive the indescribable gift of God's Son, our joyful response resulting from salvation should carry over into all areas of our life, including our giving. But when we, like Ananias and his lovely wife, Sapphira, are overcome with making the appearance of giving (Acts 5), we basically lie to God. Once we know the truth about what God expects, anything less is an abomination.

Apathy toward commitment and stewardship may be harder to overcome than a decision not to give, as this would require a change of heart and mind. It has been said that the paradox of our time in history is that we have multiplied our possessions but reduced our values. These are the days of two incomes, but more divorce; of fancier houses, but broken homes. It is a time when the show window is full, but the stockroom is empty.

A man said that he was troubled that his paycheck did not go far: "It's as if my bank account is a black hole in space. I deposit my money and it disappears. By the end of the month, it is gone. I have little to show for it; and each month, this cycle repeats." Perhaps he identified the problem without even realizing it. It is not *his* money but a trust from God. All we have comes from God and belongs to God. When we acknowledge this and are willing to be faithful stewards of the trust, God can work in concert with us to achieve life's purpose. God's economy is different from ours.

> Consider how you have fared. You have sown much, and have harvested little; you eat, but you never have enough; you drink, but never have your fill; you clothe yourselves, but no one is warm; and you that earn wages earn wages to put them into a bag with holes. (Haggai 1:5-6)

A Stewardship Faith Story

Nothing is more uplifting than hearing people tell about their personal faith journeys that have led them to a deeper understanding of God's economy. During a recent annual stewardship emphasis, a man was invited to tell about his stewardship faith story. Reluctantly, he agreed to do so, thinking that he, of all people, had little to say that would be of interest to others. He rose early on the appointed Sunday, somewhat in disbelief that he had agreed to speak publicly about his convictions, and sat quietly after breakfast pondering what he would say. At the appointed time in morning worship, he walked slowly to the microphone and began: "Friends, we have had it so good for so long that we all feel a little justified in complaining about recent economic hard times. We all know that the stock market has been in the tank for months and months. But in the context of human history, and by comparison with other peoples of the earth, we can be considered nothing but very, very rich! We are blessed, pampered, spoiled, and somewhat covetous. Covetousness is a horrible sin. Paul told the Corinthians in 1 Corinthians 5:11 that they should not 'associate with anyone who bears the name of brother or sister who is sexually immoral or greedy, or is an idolater, reviler, drunkard, or robber.' Greed—covetousness—is in pretty bad company being mentioned with immorality, idolatry, and such. Have we become so possessed by, or tolerant of, greed that it just seems out of place in that list?

"Francis de Sales heard the confessions of thousands of people—more, it has been said, than any other Catholic priest. His observations agree with those of clergy throughout the country: No one confesses to guilt of breaking the tenth commandment, 'Thou shalt not covet.' We just don't think we are guilty. Perhaps a worthy exercise would be to search our hearts with this in mind."

The man continued by saying, "Our church is in the process of underwriting our ministries to our children, youth, and adults. In a few weeks, you and I will be asked to make a decision that could change our lives. This is not life-threatening, but perhaps it is faith-threatening. God's church will continue to exist whether or not you and I successfully meet the ministry challenges that have been presented. Here's what I want to point out: The challenges we are facing don't really have much to do with underwriting an annual budget. It's much more basic than that. It's not our ability to meet these financial goals that is being challenged; it's our faith. We have heard what the Bible says about faithful stewards, and you and I have to answer the question: Do I believe that? That's what the Bible says, but do I really believe it?" Leaving the question hanging, the white-haired man walked away slowly, taking his seat beside his wife of sixty years.

Every Scripture on the subject of giving in God's economy is contrary to what the world believes, contrary to everything that seems humanly reasonable. And when we face these teachings, we have to decide if we believe these seemingly unreasonable words. It is not a challenge to our pocketbook; it is a challenge to our faith.

Chapter Fifteen

Stewardship Stories of Hope, Heart, and Happiness

Driving down the freeway, I saw a billboard caption that pretty well summarizes our work in proclaiming the message of stewardship. Paraphrased, the billboard read: "Uncertainty is a given, fear is optional." Being faithful stewards of the benefits God has graciously entrusted to us is a choice. It is akin to an evolving process, given the fact that we cannot outgive God.

Throughout the years, we have been enriched by encounters with faithful stewards. Their experiences have imprinted our stewardship ministries and perspectives along the way. This chapter is about a few of those many stories that have inspired us to reach new heights in our own personal giving and in our stewardship ministries.

The Power of Spiritual Realization

Several years ago, I was greeted in the hallway by a church member who was always supportive and encouraging, just a pleasant person. He was a wealthy man, a good steward of his wealth, and always generous. I was aware that he had made several donations to good causes in the recent past. While approaching him, I began to say, "I'm glad you're here. I intended to come see you this week to thank you for the leadership you continue to provide and for what you've done to support the work of the church. Your participation has truly made a difference in what the church has been able to accomplish."

He stopped me in mid-sentence, raising his hand to silence me and said, "Please, don't thank me for doing what gives me such great pleasure. I don't deserve any thanks. You see, I've learned the lesson of Deuteronomy 8:18."

Standing there I thought, *I can't wait to get to my Bible and look up that Scripture.* Well, I did not have to wait, since he quoted it to me: "Remember the LORD your God, for it is he who gives you power to get wealth."

Then he proceeded by saying, "I can't do a lot of things. I can't sing." (Anyone who had ever sat within ten rows of him knew that. He had volume—boy, did he have volume—though he was tone deaf.) "I can't lead a public prayer, and I can't preach. But for some reason God gave me the ability to make money."

He said, "I have no right to be arrogant about that, any more than my pastor has a right to be arrogant because he can preach a pretty good sermon. The only reason you can do what you do is because God gave you that talent. You are a steward of that talent, and you have an obligation to use it for the Lord. And the only reason I can make money is because God gave me that talent. I am a steward of that talent, and I have an obligation to use it for the Lord. I don't intend to let God down." For a person who could not preach a sermon, I think he did a pretty good job, don't you?

This man had learned a valuable lesson in life, a lesson that few people ever embrace: Money, our possession of it and the way we use it, present a tremendous challenge to us. Often, prosperity presents a challenge. The verse that my friend quoted to me is in a context that talks about the dangers of prosperity. Israel was about to cross Jordan and enter the Promised Land. Moses assembled the nation and talked to them about what they would be facing. However, he did not just talk about the giants and the walled cities; he talked about the prosperity they would experience (Deuteronomy 8:6-18). The big warning is this: When you become prosperous, unless you are careful, you will forget God.

We often admire King David because of his determination to keep God in the hearts of the people during those prosperous times in Israel. This was especially apparent in his preparations for building the Temple. For hundreds of years, the people had worshiped God in a tent. When David considered his own prosperity, that fact troubled David. He decided that they must build a more appropriate place of worship (2 Samuel 7:1-2).

When God has done so much for us, doesn't it seem only proper that we should be ill at ease unless we are doing something for God in response?

Stepping Out of Our Self-Imposed Comfort Zones

In a conference-wide capital campaign involving hundreds of churches, congregations were challenged to make a financial commitment to advance overall church growth throughout the conference. Considerable time and energy were expended communicating the missional and ministry benefits to be derived from the achievement of the goal. A primary point of the message focused on how the local congregation could make a difference by helping to extend ministry beyond its own walls.

As the campaign was midstream, a letter arrived from a small church that helped to galvanize the message of the importance of sacrificial giving. The letter said: "Enclosed is our check for $5,000. We are a struggling small church. We are not sure where the money will come from next month to pay our utility bill, but we believe so strongly in what this initiative represents that we are moved by the Spirit to make this gift." Talk about moving beyond the comfort zone. Three years later the church is thriving. God is faithful.

A Cause Greater Than Ourselves

Recently, a historical church that has been in decline for years, made the heart-wrenching decision that it must close its doors and pool efforts with other congregations in order to provide ministries to their rural community. The farming community was not experiencing growth; indeed, most of the younger people had grown up and moved away to pursue jobs elsewhere. On the final Sunday the congregation met, can you imagine the memories and sadness that pervaded the air? However, strong belief in the church's mission and trust prevailed as the church made the decision to forward the congregation's last offering to the capital campaign office with this note: "We want to give this last offering from our congregation to start new churches."

An old Marine story tells about an officer speaking to a platoon. The officer said, "Three men are needed for a dangerous mission." He knew he could simply pick out three men and order them to go; however, he decided instead to ask for volunteers: "I'm going to turn my back and give three men the opportunity to move forward one step and volunteer." He turned, waited a moment, and then faced the ranks again. A look of disappointment showed on his face. He did not see three men—not even one or two—out of rank. Before he could say anything, the sergeant spoke up: "Sir, the entire platoon has stepped forward."

With regard to embracing stewardship as a fundamental, God-given mandate, our hope is that church leaders will be committed to consistently and passionately teach and proclaim the biblical principles of stewardship.

For Further Study

More Than Money: Portraits of Transformative Stewardship, by Patrick H. McNamara (Alban Institute, 1999).

"Stewardship Stories," Appendix in *Developing a Giving Church,* by Stan Toler and Elmer Towns (Beacon Hill Press, 1999).

"Telling Stories," Chapter 8 in *Don't Shoot the Horse ('Til You Know How to Drive the Tractor): Moving From Annual Fund Raising to a Life of Giving,* by Herb Mather (Discipleship Resources, 1994).

That's What My Mother Taught Me (and Other Ways Generous Givers Develop), by Herb Mather (Discipleship Resources, 2001).

Chapter Sixteen

Final Reflections

The remaining question is, What do we do with what has been recommended? How do we take the approaches, the ideas, a new way of thinking and implement something that will result in a different experience? How do we change the paradigm of faith and money from an event to a process that nurtures and matures believers? Or, as one church planning committee asked: "What can we get away with now?" Here are some possibilities.

Equipping Clergy

Equipping and challenging clergy is a critical path. One approach is the use of a two-day retreat called a clergy think tank. This kind of retreat has been successful in a number of areas. Using ninety-minute sessions, a key question is tossed out for twelve to eighteen pastors to discuss. The facilitator provokes thought with clarifying and challenging questions and makes sure that everyone participates and that no one dominates the exchange. Resources are presented and discussed, best ideas are exchanged, problems are discussed, and faith and money is discussed in an open and encouraging way. This gives an opportunity to become aware of resources, including new books and curriculum. Knowing what others are doing also gives some clergy permission to address the subject more boldly.

A Group Training Event

Another model is for a region or group of churches to plan a training approach. In one United Methodist annual conference with nine districts, faith and money workshops were presented in two parts. The first part was to equip the clergy with an understanding of the challenge, the denominational heritage, a theology of stewardship, orientation to resources, and an open dialogue. This part was followed within a week by a second workshop for the clergy and their lay financial leaders. The same material was presented along with suggestions about various starting points. Suggestions and resources were identified for those churches that had done little with faith and money as well as for those who had been diligent in their efforts. Different levels helped the leaders identify their points of comfort for starting to change. The net result over the following two years was a measurable increase of missions giving and a number of anecdotal stories of a new day in connecting faith and money in many communities of faith.

A Local Church Design

In a local church approach, a two- or three-part design effort has been effective in many churches. After a stewardship leadership team has been appointed, an initial ninety-minute to two-hour workshop is conducted with a facilitator. The purpose is to review the challenges, the church's history, and the need for change. Then assignments are made to review some key books and resources, including videos. Analysis questions about the church may be answered before the session or by the second session. One assignment is to think of ten ways to say thank you to donors in the context of the culture of that church.

Then a second, three-hour workshop is scheduled for two or three months later. In the second workshop, the participants present their assignments and begin to plan a three-year stewardship approach. This first eighteen months includes specific month-by-month activities and assignments. Then a quarterly conceptual plan is developed for the second eighteen months.

Some groups want a third workshop to review the overall plan they have developed and to review assignments. This comprehensive plan can be reviewed by other leaders and adjusted along the way, and it provides an intentional framework to address faith and money.

A new paradigm of faith and money can result in the development of a financial master plan that addresses annual, capital, and planned giving; stewardship education for all ages; consumer education; debt counseling;

investment strategies; and financial policies. This financial master plan supports the church's strategic plan of ministry. To have one without the other is incomplete and dysfunctional. A multifaceted financial leadership team can help change the way we think about faith and money and usher in a new day of stewardship experience. This new experience is a wonderful change in thinking and practice for most churches.

It is not hard to hear angst in these pages. After many years of working with a wide variety of churches, we have developed a definite edge in our thinking. The connection between faith and money is one expression of the joy of salvation. When our convoluted and timid leadership yields to fear and defending the status quo, our salvation is diminished. Until we make the connection between faith and money, many saints will not mature in their spiritual journey. Until connecting faith and money becomes intentional in our churches, we will continue to experience incidental results. Until we fundamentally change our thinking, our communities of faith will not realize their best service.

We are tired of a *Star Wars* theology that suggests that any change and improvement in faith and money will not happen here or now, but it may happen in another church far, far away. How did we ever develop and tolerate this embracement of mediocrity? Why do we allow this recurring cycle of poverty in our attitude to reinforce a theology of scarcity? It seems that our experience is far from the admonition to give ourselves "first to the Lord" (2 Corinthians 8:5), to "strive first for the kingdom of God" (Matthew 6:33), and to give willingly and cheerfully (2 Corinthians 9:7).

Be encouraged. Connecting faith and money can lead to real revival in our hearts and minds.

Selected Biblical References for the Ministry of Stewardship Development

Generosity

Romans 12:8—The exhorter, in exhortation; the giver, in generosity; the leader, in diligence; the compassionate, in cheerfulness

2 Corinthians 8:2—For during a severe ordeal of affliction, their abundant joy and their extreme poverty have overflowed in a wealth of generosity on their part.

> **9:11**—You will be enriched in every way for your great generosity, which will produce thanksgiving to God through us.

> **9:13**—Through the testing of this ministry you glorify God by your obedience to the confession of the gospel of Christ and by the generosity of your sharing with them and with all others.

Galatians 5:22—By contrast, the fruit of the Spirit is love, joy, peace, patience, kindness, generosity, faithfulness

Generous

Exodus 35:5—Take from among you an offering to the LORD; let whoever is of a generous heart bring the LORD'S offering: gold, silver, and bronze.

Psalm 37:21—The wicked borrow, and do not pay back, but the righteous are generous and keep giving.

Proverbs 11:25—A generous person will be enriched, and one who gives water will get water.

> **19:6**—Many seek the favor of the generous, and everyone is a friend to a giver of gifts.

> **22:9**—Those who are generous are blessed, for they share their bread with the poor.

Matthew 20:15—Am I not allowed to do what I choose with what belongs to me? Or are you envious because I am generous?

Acts 2:46—Day by day, as they spent much time together in the temple, they broke bread at home and ate their food with glad and generous hearts.

2 Corinthians 8:6—So that we might urge Titus that, as he had already made a beginning, so he should also complete this generous undertaking among you.

> **8:7**—Now as you excel in everything—in faith, in speech, in knowledge, in utmost eagerness, and in our love for you—so we want you to excel also in this generous undertaking.

> **8:9**—For you know the generous act of our Lord Jesus Christ, that though he was rich, yet for your sakes he became poor, so that by his poverty you might become rich.

> **8:19**—He has also been appointed by the churches to travel with us while we are administering this generous undertaking for the glory of the Lord himself and to show our goodwill.

> **8:20**—We intend that no one should blame us about this generous gift that we are administering.

1 Timothy 6:18—They are to do good, to be rich in good works, generous, and ready to share.

James 1:17—Every generous act of giving, with every perfect gift, is from above, coming down from the Father of lights, with whom there is no variation or shadow due to change.

Gift

Genesis 33:11—"Please accept my gift that is brought to you, because God has dealt graciously with me, and because I have everything I want." So he urged him, and he took it.

Numbers 5:9—Among all the sacred donations of the Israelites, every gift that they bring to the priest shall be his.

6:14—And they shall offer their gift to the LORD, one male lamb a year old without blemish as a burnt offering, one ewe lamb a year old without blemish as a sin offering, one ram without blemish as an offering of well-being.

Proverbs 18:16—A gift opens doors; it gives access to the great.

25:14—Like clouds and wind without rain is one who boasts of a gift never given.

Ecclesiastes 5:19—Likewise all to whom God gives wealth and possessions and whom he enables to enjoy them, and to accept their lot and find enjoyment in their toil—this is the gift of God.

Matthew 5:23—So when you are offering your gift at the altar, if you remember that your brother or sister has something against you

5:24—Leave your gift there before the altar and go; first be reconciled to your brother or sister, and then come and offer your gift.

23:19—How blind you are! For which is greater, the gift or the altar that makes the gift sacred?

Acts 8:20—But Peter said to him, "May your silver perish with you, because you thought you could obtain God's gift with money!"

1 Corinthians 16:3—And when I arrive, I will send any whom you approve with letters to take your gift to Jerusalem.

2 Corinthians 8:12—For if the eagerness is there, the gift is acceptable according to what one has—not according to what one does not have.

8:20—We intend that no one should blame us about this generous gift that we are administering.

9:5—So I thought it necessary to urge the brothers to go on ahead to you, and arrange in advance for this bountiful gift that you have promised, so that it may be ready as a voluntary gift and not as an extortion.

James 1:17—Every generous act of giving, with every perfect gift, is from above, coming down from the Father of lights, with whom there is no variation or shadow due to change.

Gifts

Psalm 76:11—Make vows to the LORD your God, and perform them; let all who are around him bring gifts to the one who is awesome.

Proverbs 19:6—Many seek the favor of the generous, and everyone is a friend to a giver of gifts.

Matthew 2:11—On entering the house, they saw the child with Mary his mother; and they knelt down and paid him homage. Then, opening their treasure chests, they offered him gifts of gold, frankincense, and myrrh.

> **7:11**—If you then, who are evil, know how to give good gifts to your children, how much more will your Father in heaven give good things to those who ask him!

Luke 11:13—If you then, who are evil, know how to give good gifts to your children, how much more will the heavenly Father give the Holy Spirit to those who ask him!

> **21:1**—He looked up and saw rich people putting their gifts into the treasury.

Give

Matthew 6:2—So whenever you give alms, do not sound a trumpet before you, as the hypocrites do in the synagogues and in the streets, so that they may be praised by others. Truly I tell you, they have received their reward.

> **6:3**—But when you give alms, do not let your left hand know what your right hand is doing.

2 Corinthians 9:7—Each of you must give as you have made up your mind, not reluctantly or under compulsion, for God loves a cheerful giver.

Giving

Deuteronomy 15:4—There will, however, be no one in need among you, because the LORD is sure to bless you in the land that the LORD your God is giving you as a possession to occupy.

> **15:7**—If there is among you anyone in need, a member of your community in any of your towns within the land that the LORD your God is giving you, do not be hard-hearted or tight-fisted toward your needy neighbor.

> **15:14**—Provide liberally out of your flock, your threshing floor, and your wine press, thus giving to him some of the bounty with which the LORD your God has blessed you.

> **26:1**—When you have come into the land that the LORD your God is giving you as an inheritance to possess, and you possess it, and settle in it

> **26:2**—You shall take some of the first of all the fruit of the ground, which you harvest from the land that the LORD your God is giving you,

and you shall put it in a basket and go to the place that the LORD your God will choose as a dwelling for his name.

26:12—When you have finished paying all the tithe of your produce in the third year (which is the year of the tithe), giving it to the Levites, the aliens, the orphans, and the widows, so that they may eat their fill within your towns

2 Chronicles 30:22—Hezekiah spoke encouragingly to all the Levites who showed good skill in the service of the LORD. So the people ate the food of the festival for seven days, sacrificing offerings of well-being and giving thanks to the LORD the God of their ancestors.

Psalm 37:21—The wicked borrow, and do not pay back, but the righteous are generous and keep giving.

37:26—They are ever giving liberally and lending, and their children become a blessing.

Philippians 4:15—You Philippians indeed know that in the early days of the gospel, when I left Macedonia, no church shared with me in the matter of giving and receiving, except you alone.

James 1:17—Every generous act of giving, with every perfect gift, is from above, coming down from the Father of lights, with whom there is no variation or shadow due to change.

Greed

Job 20:20—They knew no quiet in their bellies; in their greed they let nothing escape.

Matthew 23:25—Woe to you, scribes and Pharisees, hypocrites! For you clean the outside of the cup and of the plate, but inside they are full of greed and self-indulgence.

Luke 11:39—Then the Lord said to him, "Now you Pharisees clean the outside of the cup and of the dish, but inside you are full of greed and wickedness."

12:15—And he said to them, "Take care! Be on your guard against all kinds of greed; for one's life does not consist in the abundance of possessions."

Ephesians 5:3—But fornication and impurity of any kind, or greed, must not even be mentioned among you, as is proper among saints.

Colossians 3:5—Put to death, therefore, whatever in you is earthly: fornication, impurity, passion, evil desire, and greed (which is idolatry).

1 Thessalonians 2:5—As you know and as God is our witness, we never came with words of flattery or with a pretext for greed.

2 Peter 2:3—And in their greed they will exploit you with deceptive words. Their condemnation, pronounced against them long ago, has not been idle, and their destruction is not asleep.

> **2:14**—They have eyes full of adultery, insatiable for sin. They entice unsteady souls. They have hearts trained in greed. Accursed children!

Money

2 Kings 12:4—Jehoash said to the priests, "All the money offered as sacred donations that is brought into the house of the LORD, the money for which each person is assessed—the money from the assessment of persons—and the money from the voluntary offerings brought into the house of the LORD"

> **12:7**—Therefore King Jehoash summoned the priest Jehoiada with the other priests and said to them, "Why are you not repairing the house? Now therefore do not accept any more money from your donors but hand it over for the repair of the house."

> **12:8**—So the priests agreed that they would neither accept more money from the people nor repair the house.

> **12:9**—Then the priest Jehoiada took a chest, made a hole in its lid, and set it beside the altar on the right side as one entered the house of the LORD; the priests who guarded the threshold put in it all the money that was brought into the house of the LORD.

> **12:10**—Whenever they saw that there was a great deal of money in the chest, the king's secretary and the high priest went up, counted the money that was found in the house of the LORD, and tied it up in bags.

> **12:11**—They would give the money that was weighed out into the hands of the workers who had the oversight of the house of the LORD; then they paid it out to the carpenters and the builders who worked on the house of the LORD.

> **12:13**—But for the house of the LORD no basins of silver, snuffers, bowls, trumpets, or any vessels of gold, or of silver, were made from the money that was brought into the house of the LORD.

> **12:15**—They did not ask an accounting from those into whose hand they delivered the money to pay out to the workers, for they dealt honestly.

12:16—The money from the guilt offerings and the money from the sin offerings was not brought into the house of the LORD; it belonged to the priests.

Ecclesiastes 5:10—The lover of money will not be satisfied with money; nor the lover of wealth, with gain. This also is vanity.

7:12—For the protection of wisdom is like the protection of money, and the advantage of knowledge is that wisdom gives life to the one who possesses it.

10:19—Feasts are made for laughter; wine gladdens life, and money meets every need.

Matthew 19:21—Jesus said to him, "If you wish to be perfect, go, sell your possessions, and give the money to the poor, and you will have treasure in heaven; then come, follow me."

21:12—Then Jesus entered the temple and drove out all who were selling and buying in the temple, and he overturned the tables of the money changers and the seats of those who sold doves.

25:18—But the one who had received the one talent went off and dug a hole in the ground and hid his master's money.

25:27—Then you ought to have invested my money with the bankers, and on my return I would have received what was my own with interest.

Mark 10:21—Jesus, looking at him, loved him and said, "You lack one thing; go, sell what you own, and give the money to the poor, and you will have treasure in heaven; then come, follow me."

11:15—Then they came to Jerusalem. And he entered the temple and began to drive out those who were selling and those who were buying in the temple, and he overturned the tables of the money changers and the seats of those who sold doves.

12:41—He sat down opposite the treasury, and watched the crowd putting money into the treasury. Many rich people put in large sums.

Luke 16:14—The Pharisees, who were lovers of money, heard all this, and they ridiculed him.

18:22—When Jesus heard this, he said to him, "There is still one thing lacking. Sell all that you own and distribute the money to the poor, and you will have treasure in heaven; then come, follow me."

19:15—When he returned, having received royal power, he ordered these slaves, to whom he had given the money, to be summoned so that he might find out what they had gained by trading.

19:23—Why then did you not put my money into the bank? Then when I returned, I could have collected it with interest.

John 2:14—In the temple he found people selling cattle, sheep, and doves, and the money changers seated at their tables.

2:15—Making a whip of cords, he drove all of them out of the temple, both the sheep and the cattle. He also poured out the coins of the money changers and overturned their tables.

Acts 4:37—He sold a field that belonged to him, then brought the money, and laid it at the apostles' feet.

8:18—Now when Simon saw that the Spirit was given through the laying on of the apostles' hands, he offered them money.

8:20—But Peter said to him, "May your silver perish with you, because you thought you could obtain God's gift with money!"

1 Timothy 3:3—Not a drunkard, not violent but gentle, not quarrelsome, and not a lover of money.

3:8—Deacons likewise must be serious, not double-tongued, not indulging in much wine, not greedy for money.

6:10—For the love of money is a root of all kinds of evil, and in their eagerness to be rich some have wandered away from the faith and pierced themselves with many pains.

2 Timothy 3:2—For people will be lovers of themselves, lovers of money, boasters, arrogant, abusive, disobedient to their parents, ungrateful, unholy.

Hebrews 13:5—Keep your lives free from the love of money, and be content with what you have; for he has said, "I will never leave you or forsake you."

Offering

Genesis 4:3—In the course of time Cain brought to the LORD an offering of the fruit of the ground.

4:4—And Abel for his part brought of the firstlings of his flock, their fat portions. And the LORD had regard for Abel and his offering.

4:5—But for Cain and his offering he had no regard. So Cain was very angry, and his countenance fell.

Exodus 25:2—Tell the Israelites to take for me an offering; from all whose hearts prompt them to give you shall receive the offering for me.

30:14—Each one who is registered, from twenty years old and upward, shall give the LORD'S offering.

30:15—The rich shall not give more, and the poor shall not give less, than the half shekel, when you bring this offering to the LORD to make atonement for your lives.

35:5—Take from among you an offering to the LORD; let whoever is of a generous heart bring the LORD'S offering: gold, silver, and bronze.

35:21—And they came, everyone whose heart was stirred, and everyone whose spirit was willing, and brought the LORD'S offering to be used for the tent of meeting, and for all its service, and for the sacred vestments.

35:22—So they came, both men and women; all who were of a willing heart brought brooches and earrings and signet rings and pendants, all sorts of gold objects, everyone bringing an offering of gold to the LORD.

35:24—Everyone who could make an offering of silver or bronze brought it as the LORD'S offering; and everyone who possessed acacia wood of any use in the work, brought it.

35:29—All the Israelite men and women whose hearts made them willing to bring anything for the work that the LORD had commanded by Moses to be done, brought it as a freewill offering to the LORD.

36:6—So Moses gave command, and word was proclaimed throughout the camp: "No man or woman is to make anything else as an offering for the sanctuary." So the people were restrained from bringing.

Numbers 18:26—You shall speak to the Levites, saying: When you receive from the Israelites the tithe that I have given you from them for your portion, you shall set apart an offering from it to the LORD, a tithe of the tithe.

18:28—Thus you also shall set apart an offering to the LORD from all the tithes that you receive from the Israelites; and from them you shall give the LORD'S offering to the priest Aaron.

18:29—Out of all the gifts to you, you shall set apart every offering due to the LORD; the best of all of them is the part to be consecrated.

Deuteronomy 16:10—Then you shall keep the festival of weeks for the LORD your God, contributing a freewill offering in proportion to the blessing that you have received from the LORD your God.

1 Chronicles 16:29—Ascribe to the LORD the glory due his name; bring an offering, and come before him. Worship the LORD in holy splendor.

29:14—But who am I, and what is my people, that we should be able to make this freewill offering? For all things come from you, and of your own have we given you.

29:17—I know, my God, that you search the heart, and take pleasure in uprightness; in the uprightness of my heart I have freely offered all these things, and now I have seen your people, who are present here, offering freely and joyously to you.

Psalm 54:6—With a freewill offering I will sacrifice to you; I will give thanks to your name, O Lord, for it is good.

96:8—Ascribe to the Lord the glory due his name; bring an offering, and come into his courts.

Matthew 5:23—So when you are offering your gift at the altar, if you remember that your brother or sister has something against you

Poor

Exodus 23:6—You shall not pervert the justice due to your poor in their lawsuits.

Leviticus 19:10—You shall not strip your vineyard bare, or gather the fallen grapes of your vineyard; you shall leave them for the poor and the alien: I am the Lord your God.

23:22—When you reap the harvest of your land, you shall not reap to the very edges of your field, or gather the gleanings of your harvest; you shall leave them for the poor and for the alien: I am the Lord your God.

Deuteronomy 15:11—Since there will never cease to be some in need on the earth, I therefore command you, "Open your hand to the poor and needy neighbor in your land."

24:14—You shall not withhold the wages of poor and needy laborers, whether other Israelites or aliens who reside in your land in one of your towns.

24:15—You shall pay them their wages daily before sunset, because they are poor and their livelihood depends on them; otherwise they might cry to the Lord against you, and you would incur guilt.

1 Samuel 2:8—He raises up the poor from the dust; he lifts the needy from the ash heap, to make them sit with princes and inherit a seat of honor. For the pillars of the earth are the Lord's, and on them he has set the world.

Job 20:19—For they have crushed and abandoned the poor, they have seized a house that they did not build.

24:4—They thrust the needy off the road; the poor of the earth all hide themselves.

24:9—There are those who snatch the orphan child from the breast, and take as a pledge the infant of the poor.

24:14—The murderer rises at dusk to kill the poor and needy, and in the night is like a thief.

29:12—Because I delivered the poor who cried, and the orphan who had no helper.

Psalm 9:18—For the needy shall not always be forgotten, nor the hope of the poor perish forever.

10:2—In arrogance the wicked persecute the poor—let them be caught in the schemes they have devised.

22:26—The poor shall eat and be satisfied; those who seek him shall praise the LORD. May your hearts live forever!

72:4—May he defend the cause of the poor of the people, give deliverance to the needy, and crush the oppressor.

72:12—For he delivers the needy when they call, the poor and those who have no helper.

74:19—Do not deliver the soul of your dove to the wild animals; do not forget the life of your poor forever.

74:21—Do not let the downtrodden be put to shame; let the poor and needy praise your name.

112:9—They have distributed freely, they have given to the poor; their righteousness endures forever; their horn is exalted in honor.

113:7—He raises the poor from the dust, and lifts the needy from the ash heap.

140:12—I know that the LORD maintains the cause of the needy, and executes justice for the poor.

Proverbs 13:8—Wealth is a ransom for a person's life, but the poor get no threats.

14:21—Those who despise their neighbors are sinners, but happy are those who are kind to the poor.

14:31—Those who oppress the poor insult their Maker, but those who are kind to the needy honor him.

15:15—All the days of the poor are hard, but a cheerful heart has a continual feast.

16:19—It is better to be of a lowly spirit among the poor than to divide the spoil with the proud.

17:5—Those who mock the poor insult their Maker; those who are glad at calamity will not go unpunished.

19:17—Whoever is kind to the poor lends to the LORD, and will be repaid in full.

21:13—If you close your ear to the cry of the poor, you will cry out and not be heard.

22:2—The rich and the poor have this in common: the LORD is the maker of them all.

22:9—Those who are generous are blessed, for they share their bread with the poor.

22:16—Oppressing the poor in order to enrich oneself, and giving to the rich, will lead only to loss.

22:22—Do not rob the poor because they are poor, or crush the afflicted at the gate.

28:3—A ruler who oppresses the poor is a beating rain that leaves no food.

28:6—Better to be poor and walk in integrity than to be crooked in one's ways even though rich.

28:8—One who augments wealth by exorbitant interest gathers it for another who is kind to the poor.

28:11—The rich is wise in self-esteem, but an intelligent poor person sees through the pose.

28:27—Whoever gives to the poor will lack nothing, but one who turns a blind eye will get many a curse.

31:9—Speak out, judge righteously, defend the rights of the poor and needy.

31:20—She opens her hand to the poor, and reaches out her hands to the needy.

Amos 4:1—Hear this word, you cows of Bashan who are on Mount Samaria, who oppress the poor, who crush the needy, who say to their husbands, "Bring something to drink!"

5:11—Therefore because you trample on the poor and take from them levies of grain, you have built houses of hewn stone, but you shall not live in them; you have planted pleasant vineyards, but you shall not drink their wine.

8:4—Hear this, you that trample on the needy, and bring to ruin the poor of the land

8:6—Buying the poor for silver and the needy for a pair of sandals, and selling the sweepings of the wheat

Matthew 11:5—The blind receive their sight, the lame walk, the lepers are cleansed, the deaf hear, the dead are raised, and the poor have good news brought to them.

19:21—Jesus said to him, "If you wish to be perfect, go, sell your possessions, and give the money to the poor, and you will have treasure in heaven; then come, follow me."

26:9—For this ointment could have been sold for a large sum, and the money given to the poor.

26:11—For you always have the poor with you, but you will not always have me.

Mark 10:21—Jesus, looking at him, loved him and said, "You lack one thing; go, sell what you own, and give the money to the poor, and you will have treasure in heaven; then come, follow me."

12:42—A poor widow came and put in two small copper coins, which are worth a penny.

12:43—Then he called his disciples and said to them, "Truly I tell you, this poor widow has put in more than all those who are contributing to the treasury."

14:5—"For this ointment could have been sold for more than three hundred denarii, and the money given to the poor." And they scolded her.

14:7—For you always have the poor with you, and you can show kindness to them whenever you wish; but you will not always have me.

Luke 4:18—The Spirit of the Lord is upon me, because he has anointed me to bring good news to the poor. He has sent me to proclaim release to the captives and recovery of sight to the blind, to let the oppressed go free.

6:20—Then he looked up at his disciples and said: "Blessed are you who are poor, for yours is the kingdom of God."

7:22—And he answered them, "Go and tell John what you have seen and heard: the blind receive their sight, the lame walk, the lepers are cleansed, the deaf hear, the dead are raised, the poor have good news brought to them."

14:13—But when you give a banquet, invite the poor, the crippled, the lame, and the blind.

14:21—So the slave returned and reported this to his master. Then the owner of the house became angry and said to his slave, "Go out at once into the streets and lanes of the town and bring in the poor, the crippled, the blind, and the lame."

16:20—And at his gate lay a poor man named Lazarus, covered with sores.

16:22—The poor man died and was carried away by the angels to be with Abraham. The rich man also died and was buried.

18:22—When Jesus heard this, he said to him, "There is still one thing lacking. Sell all that you own and distribute the money to the poor, and you will have treasure in heaven; then come, follow me."

19:8—Zacchaeus stood there and said to the Lord, "Look, half of my possessions, Lord, I will give to the poor; and if I have defrauded anyone of anything, I will pay back four times as much."

21:2—He also saw a poor widow put in two small copper coins.

21:3—He said, "Truly I tell you, this poor widow has put in more than all of them."

John 12:5—Why was this perfume not sold for three hundred denarii and the money given to the poor?

12:6—He said this not because he cared about the poor, but because he was a thief; he kept the common purse and used to steal what was put into it.

12:8—You always have the poor with you, but you do not always have me.

13:29—Some thought that, because Judas had the common purse, Jesus was telling him, "Buy what we need for the festival"; or, that he should give something to the poor.

Romans 15:26—Macedonia and Achaia have been pleased to share their resources with the poor among the saints at Jerusalem.

2 Corinthians 6:10—As sorrowful, yet always rejoicing; as poor, yet making many rich; as having nothing, and yet possessing everything

Galatians 2:10—They asked only one thing, that we remember the poor, which was actually what I was eager to do.

James 2:2—For if a person with gold rings and in fine clothes comes into your assembly, and if a poor person in dirty clothes also comes in

2:3—And if you take notice of the one wearing the fine clothes and say, "Have a seat here, please," while to the one who is poor you say, "Stand there," or, "Sit at my feet"

2:5—Listen, my beloved brothers and sisters. Has not God chosen the poor in the world to be rich in faith and to be heirs of the kingdom that he has promised to those who love him?

2:6—But you have dishonored the poor. Is it not the rich who oppress you? Is it not they who drag you into court?

Possessions

Matthew 19:21—Jesus said to him, "If you wish to be perfect, go, sell your possessions, and give the money to the poor, and you will have treasure in heaven; then come, follow me."

19:22—When the young man heard this word, he went away grieving, for he had many possessions.

24:47—Truly I tell you, he will put that one in charge of all his possessions.

Mark 10:22—When he heard this, he was shocked and went away grieving, for he had many possessions.

Luke 12:15—And he said to them, "Take care! Be on your guard against all kinds of greed; for one's life does not consist in the abundance of possessions."

12:33—Sell your possessions, and give alms. Make purses for yourselves that do not wear out, an unfailing treasure in heaven, where no thief comes near and no moth destroys.

12:44—Truly I tell you, he will put that one in charge of all his possessions.

14:33—So therefore, none of you can become my disciple if you do not give up all your possessions.

19:8—Zacchaeus stood there and said to the Lord, "Look, half of my possessions, Lord, I will give to the poor; and if I have defrauded anyone of anything, I will pay back four times as much."

Acts 2:45—They would sell their possessions and goods and distribute the proceeds to all, as any had need.

4:32—Now the whole group of those who believed were of one heart and soul, and no one claimed private ownership of any possessions, but everything they owned was held in common.

1 Corinthians 7:30—And those who mourn as though they were not mourning, and those who rejoice as though they were not rejoicing, and those who buy as though they had no possessions

> **13:3**—If I give away all my possessions, and if I hand over my body so that I may boast, but do not have love, I gain nothing.

Hebrews 10:34—For you had compassion for those who were in prison, and you cheerfully accepted the plundering of your possessions, knowing that you yourselves possessed something better and more lasting.

Poverty

Genesis 45:11—I will provide for you there—since there are five more years of famine to come—so that you and your household, and all that you have, will not come to poverty.

Proverbs 10:4—A slack hand causes poverty, but the hand of the diligent makes rich.

> **10:15**—The wealth of the rich is their fortress; the poverty of the poor is their ruin.

> **13:18**—Poverty and disgrace are for the one who ignores instruction, but one who heeds reproof is honored.

> **14:23**—In all toil there is profit, but mere talk leads only to poverty.

> **20:13**—Do not love sleep, or else you will come to poverty; open your eyes, and you will have plenty of bread.

> **23:21**—For the drunkard and the glutton will come to poverty, and drowsiness will clothe them with rags.

> **24:34**—And poverty will come upon you like a robber, and want, like an armed warrior.

> **28:19**—Anyone who tills the land will have plenty of bread, but one who follows worthless pursuits will have plenty of poverty.

Mark 12:44—For all of them have contributed out of their abundance; but she out of her poverty has put in everything she had, all she had to live on.

2 Corinthians 8:2—For during a severe ordeal of affliction, their abundant joy and their extreme poverty have overflowed in a wealth of generosity on their part.

> **8:9**—For you know the generous act of our Lord Jesus Christ, that though he was rich, yet for your sakes he became poor, so that by his poverty you might become rich.

Revelation 2:9—I know your affliction and your poverty, even though you are rich. I know the slander on the part of those who say that they are Jews and are not, but are a synagogue of Satan.

Rich

Exodus 30:15—The rich shall not give more, and the poor shall not give less, than the half shekel, when you bring this offering to the LORD to make atonement for your lives.

Job 34:19—Who shows no partiality to nobles, nor regards the rich more than the poor, for they are all the work of his hands

Proverbs 13:7—Some pretend to be rich, yet have nothing; others pretend to be poor, yet have great wealth.

> **22:2**—The rich and the poor have this in common: the LORD is the maker of them all.

> **22:16**—Oppressing the poor in order to enrich oneself, and giving to the rich, will lead only to loss.

> **23:4**—Do not wear yourself out to get rich; be wise enough to desist.

> **28:6**—Better to be poor and walk in integrity than to be crooked in one's ways even though rich.

> **28:20**—The faithful will abound with blessings, but one who is in a hurry to be rich will not go unpunished.

> **28:22**—The miser is in a hurry to get rich and does not know that loss is sure to come.

Matthew 19:23—Then Jesus said to his disciples, "Truly I tell you, it will be hard for a rich person to enter the kingdom of heaven."

> **19:24**—Again I tell you, it is easier for a camel to go through the eye of a needle than for someone who is rich to enter the kingdom of God.

> **27:57**—When it was evening, there came a rich man from Arimathea, named Joseph, who was also a disciple of Jesus.

Mark 10:25—It is easier for a camel to go through the eye of a needle than for someone who is rich to enter the kingdom of God.

> **12:41**—He sat down opposite the treasury, and watched the crowd putting money into the treasury. Many rich people put in large sums.

Luke 1:53—He has filled the hungry with good things, and sent the rich away empty.

6:24—But woe to you who are rich, for you have received your consolation.

12:16—Then he told them a parable: "The land of a rich man produced abundantly."

12:21—So it is with those who store up treasures for themselves but are not rich toward God.

14:12—He said also to the one who had invited him, "When you give a luncheon or a dinner, do not invite your friends or your brothers or your relatives or rich neighbors, in case they may invite you in return, and you would be repaid."

16:1—Then Jesus said to the disciples, "There was a rich man who had a manager, and charges were brought to him that this man was squandering his property."

16:19—There was a rich man who was dressed in purple and fine linen and who feasted sumptuously every day.

16:21—Who longed to satisfy his hunger with what fell from the rich man's table; even the dogs would come and lick his sores

16:22—The poor man died and was carried away by the angels to be with Abraham. The rich man also died and was buried.

18:23—But when he heard this, he became sad; for he was very rich.

18:25—Indeed, it is easier for a camel to go through the eye of a needle than for someone who is rich to enter the kingdom of God.

19:2—A man was there named Zacchaeus; he was a chief tax collector and was rich.

21:1—He looked up and saw rich people putting their gifts into the treasury.

2 Corinthians 6:10—As sorrowful, yet always rejoicing; as poor, yet making many rich; as having nothing, and yet possessing everything

1 Timothy 6:9—But those who want to be rich fall into temptation and are trapped by many senseless and harmful desires that plunge people into ruin and destruction.

6:10—For the love of money is a root of all kinds of evil, and in their eagerness to be rich some have wandered away from the faith and pierced themselves with many pains.

6:17—As for those who in the present age are rich, command them not to be haughty, or to set their hopes on the uncertainty of riches, but rather on God who richly provides us with everything for our enjoyment.

James 1:10—And the rich in being brought low, because the rich will disappear like a flower in the field

> **1:11**—For the sun rises with its scorching heat and withers the field; its flower falls, and its beauty perishes. It is the same way with the rich; in the midst of a busy life, they will wither away.

> **2:5**—Listen, my beloved brothers and sisters. Has not God chosen the poor in the world to be rich in faith and to be heirs of the kingdom that he has promised to those who love him?

> **2:6**—But you have dishonored the poor. Is it not the rich who oppress you? Is it not they who drag you into court?

> **5:1**—Come now, you rich people, weep and wail for the miseries that are coming to you.

Riches

1 Kings 3:11—God said to him, "Because you have asked this, and have not asked for yourself long life or riches, or for the life of your enemies, but have asked for yourself understanding to discern what is right,"

> **3:13**—I give you also what you have not asked, both riches and honor all your life; no other king shall compare with you.

Psalm 49:6—Those who trust in their wealth and boast of the abundance of their riches

> **52:7**—See the one who would not take refuge in God, but trusted in abundant riches, and sought refuge in wealth!

> **62:10**—Put no confidence in extortion, and set no vain hopes on robbery; if riches increase, do not set your heart on them.

> **73:12**—Such are the wicked; always at ease, they increase in riches.

> **112:3**—Wealth and riches are in their houses, and their righteousness endures forever.

Proverbs 8:18—Riches and honor are with me, enduring wealth and prosperity.

> **11:28**—Those who trust in their riches will wither, but the righteous will flourish like green leaves.

> **22:1**—A good name is to be chosen rather than great riches, and favor is better than silver or gold.

22:4—The reward for humility and fear of the LORD is riches and honor and life.

27:24—For riches do not last forever, nor a crown for all generations.

Ecclesiastes 4:8—The case of solitary individuals, without sons or brothers; yet there is no end to all their toil, and their eyes are never satisfied with riches. "For whom am I toiling," they ask, "and depriving myself of pleasure?" This also is vanity and an unhappy business.

5:13—There is a grievous ill that I have seen under the sun: riches were kept by their owners to their hurt.

5:14—And those riches were lost in a bad venture; though they are parents of children, they have nothing in their hands.

9:11—Again I saw that under the sun the race is not to the swift, nor the battle to the strong, nor bread to the wise, nor riches to the intelligent, nor favor to the skillful; but time and chance happen to them all.

1 Timothy 6:17—As for those who in the present age are rich, command them not to be haughty, or to set their hopes on the uncertainty of riches, but rather on God who richly provides us with everything for our enjoyment.

James 5:2—Your riches have rotted, and your clothes are moth-eaten.

1 John 2:16—For all that is in the world—the desire of the flesh, the desire of the eyes, the pride in riches—comes not from the Father but from the world.

Sacrifice

Romans 12:1—I appeal to you therefore, brothers and sisters, by the mercies of God, to present your bodies as a living sacrifice, holy and acceptable to God, which is your spiritual worship.

Stewards

1 Corinthians 4:1—Think of us in this way, as servants of Christ and stewards of God's mysteries.

4:2—Moreover, it is required of stewards that they be found trustworthy.

1 Peter 4:10—Like good stewards of the manifold grace of God, serve one another with whatever gift each of you has received.

Tithe

Numbers 18:21—To the Levites I have given every tithe in Israel for a possession in return for the service that they perform, the service in the tent of meeting.

18:24—I have given to the Levites as their portion the tithe of the Israelites, which they set apart as an offering to the LORD. Therefore I have said of them that they shall have no allotment among the Israelites.

18:26—You shall speak to the Levites, saying: When you receive from the Israelites the tithe that I have given you from them for your portion, you shall set apart an offering from it to the LORD, a tithe of the tithe.

Deuteronomy 12:17—Nor may you eat within your towns the tithe of your grain, your wine, and your oil, the firstlings of your herds and your flocks, any of your votive gifts that you vow, your freewill offerings, or your donations.

14:22—Set apart a tithe of all the yield of your seed that is brought in yearly from the field.

14:23—In the presence of the LORD your God, in the place that he will choose as a dwelling for his name, you shall eat the tithe of your grain, your wine, and your oil, as well as the firstlings of your herd and flock, so that you may learn to fear the LORD your God always.

14:28—Every third year you shall bring out the full tithe of your produce for that year, and store it within your towns.

26:12—When you have finished paying all the tithe of your produce in the third year (which is the year of the tithe), giving it to the Levites, the aliens, the orphans, and the widows, so that they may eat their fill within your towns

2 Chronicles 31:5—As soon as the word spread, the people of Israel gave in abundance the first fruits of grain, wine, oil, honey, and of all the produce of the field; and they brought in abundantly the tithe of everything.

31:6—The people of Israel and Judah who lived in the cities of Judah also brought in the tithe of cattle and sheep, and the tithe of the dedicated things that had been consecrated to the LORD their God, and laid them in heaps.

Nehemiah 10:38—And the priest, the descendant of Aaron, shall be with the Levites when the Levites receive the tithes; and the Levites shall bring up a tithe of the tithes to the house of our God, to the chambers of the storehouse.

13:12—Then all Judah brought the tithe of the grain, wine, and oil into the storehouses.

Malachi 3:10—Bring the full tithe into the storehouse, so that there may be food in my house, and thus put me to the test, says the LORD of hosts; see if

I will not open the windows of heaven for you and pour down for you an overflowing blessing.

Matthew 23:23—Woe to you, scribes and Pharisees, hypocrites! For you tithe mint, dill, and cummin, and have neglected the weightier matters of the law: justice and mercy and faith. It is these you ought to have practiced without neglecting the others.

Luke 11:42—But woe to you Pharisees! For you tithe mint and rue and herbs of all kinds, and neglect justice and the love of God; it is these you ought to have practiced, without neglecting the others.

Wealth

Deuteronomy 8:17—Do not say to yourself, "My power and the might of my own hand have gotten me this wealth."

> **8:18**—But remember the LORD your God, for it is he who gives you power to get wealth, so that he may confirm his covenant that he swore to your ancestors, as he is doing today.

Psalm 49:16—Do not be afraid when some become rich, when the wealth of their houses increases.

> **49:17**—For when they die they will carry nothing away; their wealth will not go down after them.

> **52:7**—See the one who would not take refuge in God, but trusted in abundant riches, and sought refuge in wealth!

Proverbs 13:11—Wealth hastily gotten will dwindle, but those who gather little by little will increase it.

Ecclesiastes 5:10—The lover of money will not be satisfied with money; nor the lover of wealth, with gain. This also is vanity.

> **5:19**—Likewise all to whom God gives wealth and possessions and whom he enables to enjoy them, and to accept their lot and find enjoyment in their toil—this is the gift of God.

> **6:2**—Those to whom God gives wealth, possessions, and honor, so that they lack nothing of all that they desire, yet God does not enable them to enjoy these things, but a stranger enjoys them. This is vanity; it is a grievous ill.

Jeremiah 9:23—Thus says the LORD: Do not let the wise boast in their wisdom, do not let the mighty boast in their might, do not let the wealthy boast in their wealth.

17:11—Like the partridge hatching what it did not lay, so are all who amass wealth unjustly; in mid-life it will leave them, and at their end they will prove to be fools.

Habakkuk 2:5—Moreover, wealth is treacherous; the arrogant do not endure. They open their throats wide as Sheol; like Death they never have enough. They gather all nations for themselves, and collect all peoples as their own.

Zephaniah 1:13—Their wealth shall be plundered, and their houses laid waste. Though they build houses, they shall not inhabit them; though they plant vineyards, they shall not drink wine from them.

Matthew 6:24—No one can serve two masters; for a slave will either hate the one and love the other, or be devoted to the one and despise the other. You cannot serve God and wealth.

13:22—As for what was sown among thorns, this is the one who hears the word, but the cares of the world and the lure of wealth choke the word, and it yields nothing.

Mark 4:19—But the cares of the world, and the lure of wealth, and the desire for other things come in and choke the word, and it yields nothing.

10:23—Then Jesus looked around and said to his disciples, "How hard it will be for those who have wealth to enter the kingdom of God!"

Luke 16:9—And I tell you, make friends for yourselves by means of dishonest wealth so that when it is gone, they may welcome you into the eternal homes.

16:11—If then you have not been faithful with the dishonest wealth, who will entrust to you the true riches?

16:13—No slave can serve two masters; for a slave will either hate the one and love the other, or be devoted to the one and despise the other. You cannot serve God and wealth.

18:24—Jesus looked at him and said, "How hard it is for those who have wealth to enter the kingdom of God!"

Acts 19:25—These he gathered together, with the workers of the same trade, and said, "Men, you know that we get our wealth from this business."

2 Corinthians 8:2—For during a severe ordeal of affliction, their abundant joy and their extreme poverty have overflowed in a wealth of generosity on their part.

Give Thanks / Thanks Giving
    to God   by what we give

- Background of the song
- Give thanks to whom?
        ~~for~~ what?
    How?

Covet?

Spend even less making money — for what?

Mission
    → purpose of the church — equip to live & serve
                         a   a world in need
                            fuel
                      God-breathed life

Enneagram:

Carl Jung   9 with a 1 wing

Pope John ~~XXIII~~

Gandhi

Parker Palmer

Bill Clinton